# THE DORDOGNE REGION OF FRANCE

*IAN SCARGILL*

DAVID & CHARLES

NEWTON ABBOT   LONDON

NORTH POMFRET (VT)   VANCOUVER

0 7153 6659 9

To Mary

Set in 11 on 13pt Baskerville and printed in
Great Britain by Latimer Trend & Company Ltd Plymouth
for David & Charles (Holdings) Limited
South Devon House   Newton Abbot   Devon

Published in the United States of America by
David & Charles Inc   North Pomfret
Vermont 05053   USA

Published in Canada by Douglas David &
Charles Limited   3645 McKechnie Drive
West Vancouver BC

# CONTENTS

# ILLUSTRATIONS

PLATES

*Photographs other than those acknowledged are by the author*

## MAPS AND DIAGRAMS

# 1 FOUR RIVERS AND FOUR BARONS

THERE can be few words quite so evocative of French life and landscape as *Dordogne.* The mental picture that it conjures up will be composed of many images, of *pâté de foie gras* and truffles, of caves and wall paintings, of fortified towns and village fêtes. It is certain to include a river scene, perhaps one of those memorable views of the great castle of Beynac on its high crag above the Dordogne, or of the abbey at Brantôme reflected in the clear waters of the Dronne. It is entirely appropriate that the picture should include rivers because it is to its four principal rivers that this region of France owes its historic unity, and it is upon the valleys that the activity of the region has always focused.

To the Frenchman the word *Dordogne* is likely to have a more prosaic meaning. To him it is an administrative unit, one of the ninety-five *départements* into which France is divided for purposes of local government and recognised by the number 24 on the postmark of an envelope or the registration plate of a motor car. The Frenchman is no less fond of the Dordogne region than the growing number of English and other foreigners who visit this part of France each year, nor does he lack imagination when recalling the pleasures of a holiday spent here, but to evoke the same images in his mind it is preferable to use the word *Périgord.*

This book is about Périgord, an ancient territory, the boundaries of which correspond very closely with those of the modern *département* of Dordogne. Indeed it is historical continuity that forms one of the principal themes of the book. As Daniel Faucher, the French geographer, observed 'Périgord is more easily defined in terms of history and tradition than by geography'. In what follows, the term *Périgord* will generally be preferred to the less precise *Dordogne* or *Dordogne region*, but except where Dordogne is used with specific reference to the river, the three should be regarded as synonymous.

As Faucher's comment implies, Périgord is not easy to recognise on a road map of France, or even a topographic atlas. It lies to the north-east of Bordeaux and extends inland nearly as far as Brive and Limoges. Périgueux, the 'county' town, is almost exactly at the centre. It is transitional in geology and relief between the bleak uplands of the Massif Central to the east and the marshy coastlands around the estuary of the Garonne and Dordogne rivers. From the north-east, where crystalline plateaux like those of neighbouring Limousin rise to about 500 metres, the general slope of the land is towards the south-west and the broad alluvial valley of the Dordogne below Bergerac is no more than a few metres above sea-level and the countryside begins to resemble that around Bordeaux and Agen. To the east and south-east there are arid limestone landscapes that remind one of the *Causses* of nearby Quercy, whilst low, rounded hills in the north-west merge imperceptibly into those of the adjacent Charente country, or Angoumois.

It will be evident from these few comments that the Dordogne region possesses little physical unity, indeed it is far more accurately described as one of transition. The same characteristic applies to its climate and also to the use which man has been able to make of the land. Stock-rearing and dairying are associated increasingly with the higher plateaux, especially to the north, whilst the milder, sunnier conditions of the valleys and river basins encourage viticulture and the cultivation of maize, tobacco, fruits and nuts. But physical contrasts also occur over very short distances and the peasant farmer has traditionally exploited these local differences in rocks, relief and climate to grow the variety of crops that has long been a feature of the life of this region.

Yet Périgord is not without some measure of physical unity, such unity as it possesses deriving in part from its geological make-up but, still more, from its river system. Rocks range in age from the ancient granites and schists that are a part of the Massif Central to Tertiary sands and clays comparable with those of the Landes, the forested plains south of Bordeaux. They also include Liassic clays and Jurassic limestones like those of the Causses. Nevertheless something like half the total area of the region, including the whole of its central part, is composed of rocks of Middle and Upper Cretaceous age, mainly limestones, and the broad limestone plateau, deeply dissected by wide river valleys, can be regarded as the most common element in the physical geography of Périgord.

That is not to say that the limestones are everywhere exposed at the surface, for large parts of the region, especially the centre and south, have a patchy covering of much younger sands and gravels. Where these occur, typically capping the upper slopes, they are usually under woodland and there are some extensive forests between the main river valleys, recognised by their local names: Forêt de Liorac, Forêt de Feytaud, etc. More than a quarter of Périgord is forested and it will be pointed out that the history of the region cannot be understood without reference to the role of the forest in the life of its people.

It is to its river system that Périgord principally owes its unity. Flowing across different geological outcrops the rivers serve to unite contrasting physical units or *pays*, their valleys having long served as routeways, facilitating the exchange of goods between these pays and assisting the movement of people and ideas, bringing about social and political as well as economic unity. Périgord is well described as consisting of:

> . . . little local cells united by the confluence of valleys, too small and too incomplete in themselves to remain isolated, but by their association together, comprising a political and social entity with a life of its own.                    Paul Fénelon

Most of the region's drainage is collected by four rivers, the Dronne, Isle, Vézère and Dordogne. A quick glance at a map might suggest that each follows a roughly parallel course from north-east to south-west, but in detail this is far from correct and a more accurate and meaningful interpretation of the map is one which regards the river Isle as a kind of master stream to which the life of the other valleys is directed. Tributary valleys provide linking routeways. The Dronne and the Isle are only a few kilometres apart at Tocane-Saint-Apre but communication between them is made even easier by the low divides at Mensignac and La Chapelle-Gonaguet. From the Isle near Périgueux the valley of the Manoire conducts important routeways towards the Vézère. The route to Les Eyzies is a particularly impressive corridor used not only by a road but by a railway which descends to the Vézère by the valley provided by the Manaurie stream. Similarly the N21, which carries heavy road traffic between Périgueux and Bergerac, makes use of the Caudeau valley for its long descent to the Dordogne. As the sketch map demonstrates (Fig 1), the pattern of river valleys provides a system of routeways which focuses on the middle Isle valley at Périgueux. Herein lies another clue to the region's history.

Périgord is a land of four rivers; in pre-Roman times it was the home of four native tribes; in the Middle Ages it was split into four baronies; and the modern *département* is divided for administrative convenience into four *arrondissements*. Whatever the form of division, however, the several parts have always looked to the middle Isle valley as a focus of organisation and authority.

The Romans, who entered the region in 56 BC, encountered four native clans, the *Petro-corii*, from the name of which it is an easy step to the modern Périgord. These Gaulish tribes, their respective territories probably centred on the four major river valleys, seem to have been grouped in a kind of federation which looked to the central settlement of Vesunna (later Périgueux) as their territorial headquarters. This settlement, or oppidum, was on the south bank of the Isle where two hills afforded an easily defensible site, though most of the later development of the town was to take place on the opposite bank. Thus from very early times one finds a town in the middle Isle valley acting as a centre of regional activity. Périgueux has played this role ever since.

Under Roman rule a new settlement was founded on the north bank of the river and the territory administered from this new site became in due time the diocese of Périgueux, the administrative organisation of the Church reinforcing that established under earlier military control. In 1317 the diocese was divided when Pope John XXII created a new diocese of Sarlat, but the two together, Périgueux and Sarlat, retained the outline of the older territory and the unity which religious organisation and discipline imposed, enabled this territory— Périgord—to survive the political fragmentation that took place in the Middle Ages. The two dioceses were reunited after the Revolution.

During the early Middle Ages the region retained a measure of political unity as the *Comté de Périgord*, but the overlordship of this territory was weak and local rulers exercised a good deal of power. Under the comte, authority was divided between four powerful baronies—those of Mareuil, Bourdeilles, Beynac and Biron—whose rulers, jealous of each other's power, built strong castles and conducted almost constant warfare amongst themselves. In turn their vassals fought one another, building more castles. Medieval skirmishing cannot have made life easy for the peasant population but it left the Dordogne more richly endowed with castles and fortified churches than any other part of France.

The centuries up to the Revolution were marked by almost continual affrays punctuated by devastating wars, and land regularly changed hands. Yet remarkably a sense of the historic unity of Périgord survived, due both to the role of the Church and to long-standing economic ties, so that when, in 1790, the *département* of Dordogne was created as one of the eighty-three political divisions of France which existed at that time, its boundaries corresponded surprisingly closely with those of the ancient diocese. The *préfecture*, administrative headquarters of the new *département*, was established at Périgueux, the geographical centre and point of maximum accessibility.

Périgueux remains the administrative, commercial and industrial hub of the Dordogne but some of these functions are shared with a number of other towns, principally Bergerac, Sarlat, Nontron and Ribérac. Each of these exercises its own attraction over the surrounding villages and smaller towns, most evident on market day, and this role is recognised in names that are in common usage for the areas served by the towns: the Bergeracois, Sarladais, Nontronnais and Ribéracois. Indefinite as to boundaries, these units correspond to some degree with older divisions of ancient Périgord, and loosely, even, with its physical divisions. At this level too, there is continuity with the past.

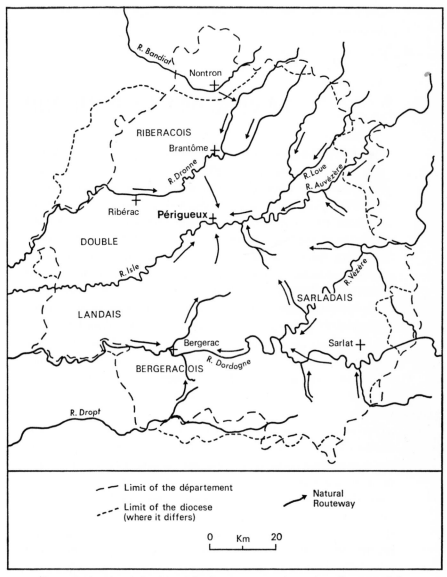

Fig 1 Périgord: relationship of the département to the ancient diocese, and the centralising influence of natural routeways (after Paul Fénelon, *Le Périgord: Étude Morphologique*)

ACASUAL glance from a hilltop near Périgueux, Sarlat or Ribérac would reveal little to excite the imagination. In every direction the generally accordant summits of the hills give an impression of flatness, of monotony, and the woodland that covers many of these higher portions of the region, heightens the feeling that this is a dull and uninviting landscape. Such a glance, in fact, provides no clue to the remarkable variety of relief forms that lie beneath the ancient planation surfaces that the hilltops represent. Even where lime stones predominate, as they often do over more than half the region, there are contrasts depending upon the composition of the rock and its resistance to erosion. In places there are rounded hills reminiscent of the downlands of southern England, elsewhere bare karstic surfaces or miniature 'wealds' where anticlinal domes have been breached to reveal older, more varied rocks, within their core.

Périgord also includes, in the north-east, a portion of the Massif Central, and the massive forms in the crystalline rocks of the Nontronnais and Lanouaille are as different as they could be from the finely chiselled features of the Bergeracois, or the more flowing landscapes of the Double and the Landais carved out of the much younger sediments which fringe the region in the south-west and extend across its border into Agenais and the Bordelais. But the glory of Périgord lies in its valleys and especially those of its principal rivers, the Dronne, the Isle, the Vézère and the Dordogne. Here gorges alternate with fertile basins, sharp meanders with gentle curves, and their banks are

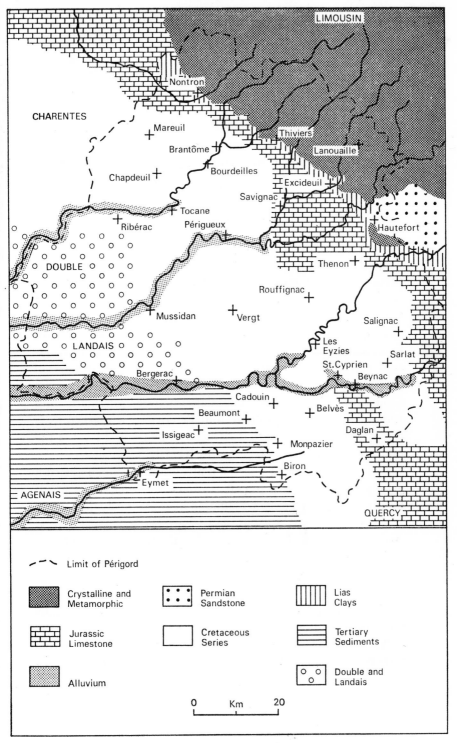

Fig 2   Périgord: geology

frequently bordered with cliffs which overhang and hide the caves which provided a home for the earliest inhabitants of the region. The valleys have always been more attractive to man than the neighbouring uplands—'ribbons of water and of light'—and the life and activity which is concentrated in them is in contrast with the wooded hills, places of solitude and retreat.

### THE NONTRONNAIS

Journeying north on the N675 from Brantôme, a traveller cannot fail to be impressed by the sudden change of scenery that takes place after passing through Nontron. A similar change can be observed on the N21 after Thiviers or the N704 north of Cubas. Beyond each of these little market towns the road rises sharply to a countryside that has more in common with parts of Brittany or Cornwall than with the rest of Périgord. Geologically it is a part of the Massif Central, the crystalline uplands of central France, and it is continued north-eastwards in the Limousin. The historic boundary between Périgord and Limousin, between Petrocorii and Lemovices, is marked by a range of quartzitic hills that rise above the general level of the plateau to some 500 to 550 metres (Courbefy 551 metres).

Below these rounded hills is a plateau surface, much of it at a general height of 350 to 400 metres above sea-level, its smoothed nature owing much to peneplanation in former geological times. But deeply incised into the plateau are the valleys of several rivers—Auvézère, Loue, Isle, Côle, Dronne and Bandiat—which often flow 150 to 200 metres below the general level of the plateau, valley and upland thus standing in sharp contrast with each other.

Upland scenery is massive and uncomplicated, owing its uniformity to the compact and homogeneous nature of the rocks, mostly granites or metamorphic gneisses and schists. Granite outcrops extensively to the north of Nontron and again

18

in the vicinity of Excideuil. Between these two is a broad exposure of metamorphic rocks, but in their generally crystalline nature and in their resistance to erosion, there is little difference between the various rock types and it is their general hardness that has contributed to the preservation of old planation surfaces. Broadly speaking the granite may be said to give rise to a more rounded form of upland than the gneiss which is characterised to a greater extent by flat plateau tops and abrupt edges overlooking the valleys. But there are exceptions even to this generalisation, the highly compressed granites of part of the Excideuil massif, for example, outcropping in the form of flat, slab-like blocks.

In places the granite is mantled with a layer of weathered mineral debris, mostly quartz which has been left as a result of the decomposition of the felspar and mica. This mantle of waste contributes to the smoothed profile of the granitic uplands and it serves to protect the underlying rocks from further erosion since rainwater is absorbed by the rotted debris. Occasionally, where the mantle has been partly eroded, resistant blocks of unweathered granite are exposed or left scattered over the surface. At Saint-Estèphe, north of Nontron, they form a curious arrangement of blocks, known popularly as the *Chapelet du Diable*—the devil's rosary.

The streams which rise on the crystalline plateaux flow first in broad, gentle-sided hollows. They tend to radiate from the higher upland shoulders but in places where the surface is very flat the drainage is immature, the ground swampy and small lakes form. But lower down, where several streams unite, they become deeply incised in valleys which may be straight or may display broad, meandering forms. The latter are most typical where the make-up of the rocks is most varied. The really impressive gorges, however, are those of the rivers which rise outside the region and so have begun to achieve their gorge-like sections by the time they enter it. Valley bottoms are stony, often littered with fallen granite blocks and boulders, and the rivers tumble over many small waterfalls and rapids. They are strikingly picturesque, contrasting with the sober forms of the higher plateaux. During the eighteenth and early nineteenth centuries there was a flourishing iron industry in these valleys, furnaces and forges being set up to take advantage of the natural power sites and of the ores and charcoal that could be obtained nearby (page 80).

A damp climate, at least in comparison with the rest of Périgord, and soils that are frequently cold, heavy and acidic, mean that the crystalline uplands of the Nontronnais have never been very attractive to arable farming. They are seen at their most uninviting beyond Miallet and La Coquille where thin soils developed on granulite and gneiss support a very scanty population and there are extensive tracts of chestnut wood and heaths of gorse and heather (*brandes*). But where the soils have been lightened and fertilised they are capable of yielding good crops of wheat and potatoes and, in sharp contrast with the bleak uplands just described, there is the country around Lanouaille where deeply weathered mica schists have given rise to easily worked and fertile soils which support quite a dense farming population. Between these extremes, the countryside is most typically one of grass or woodland, in places almost parkland in appearance. Meat, milk and young livestock are produced, and the practise is long-standing by which the products of this area are exchanged with those of other parts of Périgord further south. This need for exchange explains the presence of small market towns that have grown up along the line of contact. Away from the zone of contact, the density of population varies considerably.

It is not unusual these days to hear the Nontronnais referred to as *Périgord Vert*, a title that is meant to be descriptive of the woods and pastures of this well-watered pays. As a local name, however, Périgord Vert has less tradition behind it and is less authentic than the terms *Périgord Blanc* and *Périgord Noir*, associated respectively with the Ribéracois and the Sarladais.

At least one authority on the history of Périgord has dismissed it scornfully as a twentieth-century invention of the Syndicats d'Initiative of the Nontronnais district. Are the forests of north-eastern Périgord any greener than those of the centre or the south?

### THE FRINGING BASINS

The edge of the granite uplands is marked by a narrow strip of lowland which takes the form of a series of small basins joined together by low divides and it is in these lowland basins that most of the small market centres are situated. The divides have been utilised by roads and by a railway that winds its way from Nontron to Hautefort, linking the towns and facilitating their trade.

The basins correspond with outcrops of soft Liassic clays and marls or, further south around Hautefort and Terrasson, of a crumbly, red Permian sandstone. Impermeable for the most part, these rocks have offered little resistance to erosion and have been hollowed out by numerous little streams forming depressions. Typical examples can be seen at Saint-Martial-de-Valette near Nontron, at Saint-Pardoux on the Dronne or at Saint-Jean-de-Côle, Corgnac, Excideuil and Cherveix. But the rocks are by no means absolutely uniform in their durability and harder bands intrude to form minor scarps and flat-topped hills, and the scenery of the basins is thus a pleasantly varied one. A common feature where the Permian rocks outcrop is a low hill with a capping of harder oolitic limestone and both Hautefort and the nearby market centre of Badefols-d'Ans stand on platforms of this kind.

Owing to their lower altitude, the climate experienced in these lowland basins is both warmer and drier than that of the plateaux to north and south. This makes it possible to grow crops such as vines and tobacco, more typical of the bigger valleys further south. Walnuts are of special importance and the richer farming of which they form the basis has contributed to the prosperity of a large number of settlements. In contrast with the adjoining plateaux, the basins earn the title of *bons pays*.

Overlooking the fertile clay basins in the west is a discontinuous escarpment which marks the easternmost limit of the limestone hill and plateau country of central Périgord. This scarp feature is rarely more than 30 to 40 metres high and in places it disappears altogether because the rocks of which it is composed are of varying hardness. Where it is present, though, it offers some superb views towards the high plateaux further east, as from the D61/D60 which follows the escarpment northwards from the Dordogne through Carlux and Salignac, picturesque villages situated in relation to gaps in the ridge.

From the scarp westwards the view appears less exciting, accordant summit levels and wooded hilltops giving the impression of monotony to which reference was made above. But the superficiality of the impression is soon revealed when one penetrates the limestone country. An enormous variety of relief forms present themselves, and at once a distinction must be made between the landscapes typical, on the one hand, of the rocks of Jurassic age and, on the other, of the younger Cretaceous sediments. In contrast with the landforms of the crystalline Nontronnais or those associated with the molasses of the Bergeracois, some of the differences are ones of degree rather than kind. Nevertheless a broad distinction can be made between the more rounded hill forms typical of the Cretaceous rocks, and the harsher, flatter surfaces of the Jurassic limestones. The latter are less extensive in their outcrop than the former, frequently appearing only as a narrow belt in the east, but there is one locality where the outcrop broadens out to form a small Causse, the landscape of which is more reminiscent of the Causses of nearby Quercy than of the rest of Périgord.

The Causse of Périgord lies to the east of Périgueux and is delimited very approximately by lines joining that town, Thiviers and Thenon. On a map it can be picked out at once by the general absence of surface drainage, although the Isle and the Auvézère cross it in deeply incised valleys and the surface is scored by numerous dry valleys which once held permanent streams. Away from the two rivers, much of the Causse is a flat-topped plateau at some 200 to 220 metres above sea-level, but diversified here and there by knobbly hills composed of a harder, oolitic limestone which protrude up to 50 metres above this general level. The plateau is grey, bare and uninviting and stones frequently litter the surface. In places these are piled together in heaps known locally as *queyrous*, and the lower slopes of the dry valleys are often made up of scree material, fallen blocks and stones. To the novelist, Eugène Le Roy, the Causse was 'Le Pays des Pierres'—The Land of Stones.

In places the plateaux are pitted with hollows resulting from the solution of the limestone. But most of the precipitation quickly finds its way through the fissures in this very permeable rock so that the surface is dry and parts are entirely devoid of vegetation. Where it does grow, the natural vegetation tends to be scrub-like with juniper bushes, brambles and stunted oaks (*garrisades*) which have little value except as a source of truffles. The Causse has a stark beauty and is fascinating to the natural historian, but from the farmer's point of view it is a poor and unattractive country and much depopulation has taken place making this one of the most thinly peopled areas of Périgord.

Where cereal crops have been grown, these have usually been of rye and oats rather than wheat or barley, but returns are meagre and farmland has tended to be abandoned. Vines were once grown quite extensively, but little attempt was made to reintroduce them after the vineyards were devastated by phylloxera (aphids which destroy the roots), and even the truffle oaks which were planted to replace the vines in some parts have had a struggle to survive. In contrast with the

23

generally unrewarding plateaux, however, the two river valleys introduce an element of almost oasis-like prosperity as is apparent from the much larger number of settlements. Wheat and maize, walnuts and tobacco are grown where there is sufficient land but certain sections of the valleys are too gorge-like to permit more than a very little cultivation.

South of the Dordogne, around Daglan and Campagnac, there is a small extension of the Causse of Quercy where the physical conditions are very similar to those described above.

## THE HEART OF PÉRIGORD

Sedimentary rocks of Middle and Upper Cretaceous age out-crop over a broad band of country from the borders of Angoumois in the north-west to the Sarladais in the south-east, and give rise to what must be regarded as the most typical scenery of the region.

The rocks which make up the Cretaceous series are much more varied in their composition than those of the Causse and although calcareous beds tend to predominate, these are generally much thinner than the massive limestones of Jurassic age. Furthermore, even the calcareous bands vary considerably in their resistance to erosion, some of them resisting the weathering process to form cliffs and escarpments, others breaking down easily under the action of frost and running water to yield ultimately only a residue of sandy or clay debris which fills the valley bottoms. Intercalated amongst the calcareous beds are sandstones and clay facies, indicating that the Cretaceous rocks were formed under shallow sea conditions and this conclusion is borne out by the presence here and there of coarse materials of deltaic origin and even of thin seams of lignite, a poor quality coal. Not only do the rocks exhibit rapid variations in vertical section but they also change laterally over relatively short distances, beds thinning out and disappearing to be succeeded by rocks of quite different composition.

24

The solid rocks are also covered in places with superficial deposits, remains of a hard, lateritic layer (the *Sidérolithique*) which probably resulted from decomposition of the Cretaceous rocks *in situ*, and of younger sands, gravels and clays brought and deposited by rivers draining the uplands further east after the period of Tertiary mountain-building. The terms 'Siderolithic Sands' or 'Périgord Sands' are often used interchangeably to describe the deposits as a whole. They are reddish-brown in colour and include pebbles and hard, concretionary nodules of sandstone as well as fine sands. They have a high iron content. Given this heterogeneity of rock type, both solid and superficial, it is not surprising that in detail the physical forms of both hills and valleys should be as diverse as they are.

Despite the range of both rocks and landforms, however, it is possible to distinguish a number of sub-regions where a particular type of physical landscape may, with reservations, be regarded as 'typical'. In particular a broad distinction can be made between the Ribéracois centred on the river Dronne in the north, central Périgord around Périgueux and the middle Isle valley, and the Sarladais which looks to the Vézère and nearby portions of the Dordogne valley.

The Ribéracois is often referred to as *Périgord Blanc*, a name deriving from the frequent outcrops of a chalky limestone (*Marnes Campaniennes*) which impart whitish tints to the landscape. It is a more open country than the remainder of Périgord, less forested and with distant views. The chalk hills, rarely rising to more than 200 metres, display typically rounded forms. Their broad swells are not unlike those of the downlands of southern England although their land-use and settlement obscures the comparison. The convexity of the upper slopes owes much to the porosity of the rock whilst the concave lower slopes have been smoothed by the accumulation of fine material washed down under the colder and wetter climatic conditions of post-glacial times. At the foot of these long and gentle slopes are rich-looking valleys, marshy in places and often lined with

25

poplars. Collecting most of this drainage is the Dronne, between Brantôme and Ribérac, surely one of the most beautiful valleys in the whole of France. In the nineteenth century these rounded hills of the Ribéracois were given over extensively to the vine from which both wines and liqueurs were made for sale. But only limited replanting took place after phylloxera had destroyed the vineyards and today agriculture is devoted increasingly to grain ('the granary of Périgord') and livestock production.

In contrast with the generally light tones of the Ribéracois, those of the Sarladais are dark and sombre earning its title of *Périgord Noir*. The dark shades are a product not so much of the rocks directly as of the forest which covers wide tracts of country, woods principally of oak, chestnut and pine with juniper and other scrub vegetation. Extensive woodland usually denotes sandy soils and although the underlying rock is generally a sandy limestone (*Grés Calcaires*) this is widely covered with siderolithic sands, the residual deposits referred to above. When it is present the sandy covering gives a rounded profile to the hilltops which is in sharp contrast with the abrupt edges and angular sections of the valleys. The latter owe their angularity to the fact that the main scarp-forming rock is a much purer limestone which is underlain by clay. Erosion causes the limestone to overhang or fall in huge blocks to the valley below.

A strange, but characteristic landscape feature of the Sarladais, is the *pech*, a low tabular hill resembling the base of a sawn-off cone. They are most common to the east of Sarlat and Domme where they project some 30 to 40 metres above the general level of the countryside, often enclosing small basins, known locally as *plaines*. The latter may be a couple of kilometres in diameter, as at Manobre and La Canéda, and are floored with fine sands. The pechs give an unreal, almost fantastic appearance to the landscape in places. They have been preserved from erosion because the rock of which they are composed is a hard dolomitic limestone and they may be covered with woodland or, where they are lower, be under farmland.

As in the Ribéracois, the hills of the Sardalais were devoted more widely to the vine in the past, but many vineyards were never replaced after the phylloxera. In the more wooded parts, for example to the west of Sarlat, the population density is very low, resembling that of the arid Causse and the emptiness of these parts contrasts with the life and activity of the river valleys and the fertile *plaines*.

The scenery of central Périgord is less distinctive than that of the Ribéracois to the north or of the Sarladais to the south, and includes elements that have been singled out as typical of both these other areas. In the Vern valley to the south-west of Périgueux, for example, there is a downland landscape reminiscent of that further north, whilst the Forêt Barade to the east of the town is like the Sarladais, thinly populated with forest growing on the sandy cappings of the hills. Central Périgord, in common with both the other two sub-regions, exhibits examples of karst landforms, resulting from the solution and erosion of the limestone, and something must be said about the three more common forms which the destruction of the limestone takes. These are *combes* (dry valleys), *crozes* (solution hollows) and *grottes* (underground caverns).

Dry valleys, though not as deep or as branching as those of the Causse, are nevertheless a common feature wherever limestones outcrop. They are referred to as combes, but locally this name may be restricted to the upper part of the valley where it widens out to form a broad hollow, scalloping the edge of the plateau above and ending in a steep back wall or *bout du monde* ('end of the world'). The lower portion of the valley is usually occupied with deposits of sand and clay that have been left after the solution of the impure limestones above. An underground stream may flow beneath the floor of the valley, which in wet seasons breaks out at the surface. It is claimed that water flowing underground can sometimes be heard from the surface

27

and the experienced farmer will listen and know where to sink his well. Permanent risings have had an important part to play, not only in helping to determine the site of settlements, but in powering watermills and in providing water for the irrigation of meadows and orchards.

Solution hollows are to be found on the plateau and hilltops where permeating rainwater has widened the joints in the rock and solution from below has eventually led to collapse of the surface layer. The name *croze* is derived from *cro*, meaning hole, and the solution hollow represents an initial stage in the formation of a combe which takes place by coalescence of these depressions. Other names are used to describe the same landforms elsewhere in France, *cloup* in Quercy, in other parts *igue* or *doline*. Usually they are no more than 50 metres in diameter and they may be about 10 metres deep but this latter figure is misleading because although the bottom of the solution hollow may be filled with boulders, there is a neck or narrow passage (*aven*) below which conducts the rainwater to what may be an intricate system of underground caverns.

Skilled cavers can usually find their way by the narrowest of passages to the grottes below, but occasionally the communicating aven is wide and facilities are available for the uninitiated visitor to descend. Such is the case at the Gouffre de Proumeyssac near Le Bugue in the valley of the Vézère, a smaller version of the famous Gouffre de Padirac in the Causse de Gramat. *Gouffre* is the word used to describe a cavern with a wide opening to the surface, but not all grottes communicate so directly with the surface. This is true of many of the underground caverns in the vicinity of Les Eyzies where access is from various points on the cliffs. Caves are numerous in this particular part of Périgord because of the purity of the limestone and many of them exhibit the bizarre formations created by stalactites and stalagmites. Best known of these is the Grotte du Grand Roc near Les Eyzies but there are several others that can be visited in the same locality.

In the past the underground caverns have served as a place of refuge for man from his enemies or from wild beasts such as wolves, and over a hundred caves have been identified in Périgord that were once occupied. They are generally known as *clusels* or *cluseaux*. Some of the caves contain workable mineral deposits which accumulated in them when enormous post-glacial rivers scoured the crystalline uplands to the east. China clay, for example, has been worked in caves at Roumayères for use in the porcelain industry at Limoges.

The glacially swollen rivers, charged with debris, enlarged some caves and destroyed others. It doesn't require an enormous stretch of imagination to picture some of the cliff sections, especially those in the Vézère valley, as the walls of former caverns. But other influences, too, have shaped both the form and the direction of the river valleys and it is to the effect of one of these, structural dislocation, that attention must be turned next.

Although the principal valleys of the region tend to follow a direction that is, broadly speaking, north-east/south-west, this is not true of all sections of their courses. Careful study of the map will not only confirm this fact but will show that many of the minor, tributary streams do, in fact, flow in a direction that is at right angles to that of the main rivers, that is from north-west to south-east or vice versa. Their valleys, like that of the Manoire, are the ones that have proved so valuable to man as routeways linking the major valley axes. The explanation lies in the presence of folds and faults which cut across the grain of the country creating zones of weakness in the rocks which have been picked out by the rivers and smaller streams.

In places the crest of an anticlinal fold has been worn away to reveal older and possibly softer rocks in the centre and an example of what is called 'inverted relief' is produced, that is to say the present valley coincides with what was originally the crest of the anticline. This is so at Mareuil in the north of Périgord where the valley of the river Belle—followed by the N139

29

from Angoulême—coincides with an anticlinal fold. An even better example can be seen a few kilometres to the south at La Tour Blanche. Here it is possible to stand on the edge of an inward-facing escarpment, the eroded flank of the anticline, and look across the hollowed-out core of the fold to the corresponding scarp on the other side. The rock forming the encircling escarpment is a pure white limestone, easily worked as a building stone when it is first exposed in a quarry, but hardening like marble when revealed to the atmosphere for any length of time. The softer rocks within the anticlinal fold have been worn away by the little rivers Euche and Ruche, their direction coinciding with the fold axis. Erosion has proceeded so far, however, that at the heart of the anticline an older series of limestones, of Jurassic age, have been exposed and these protrude as low hills within the eroded basin. The villages of Chapdeuil, Saint-Just and Cercles have been built on the slopes of these hills, avoiding the damp valley floors.

As well as guiding the courses of many minor streams, fold and fault structures also account for some sudden changes in the direction of flow of the main rivers, for example of the Dronne just above Brantôme, of the Isle at Périgueux and of the Dordogne which pursues a highly erratic course between Domme and Siorac where it crosses the axis of several parallel fold structures.

Characteristic of the bigger valleys is an alternation of narrow gorge-like sections with small basins or stretches of broad, open valley. Furthermore valley sides exhibit contrasted forms, even within what are predominantly gorge sections. Within their valleys the rivers also follow what, in detail, may appear to be a highly capricious course, here flowing absolutely straight, there performing an intricate series of meander loops. Such contrasts, all of which may be observed within a single short section, have established the reputation of these river valleys as amongst the most beautiful and fascinating in France.

The alternation of basin and gorge owes something to the

structural controls, folds and faults, referred to above, but a part of the explanation lies also in the contrasted nature of the rocks over which the rivers flow, some offering considerable resistance to erosion whilst others are far more easily worn away. The basins provide good opportunities for agriculture, their alluvial soils and warm, sheltered climate attracting settlement to them. Early man may of necessity have preferred the shelter of caves in the gorge sections, but most of the present-day villages or small market towns are set amongst the cultivated slopes in the valley basins. Numerous examples can be found. Note on a topographic map the position of Montignac in a valley basin above the long gorge section of the Vézère and of Le Bugue and Saint-Cirq below it, of Lisle in the Dronne valley below the gorge around Bourdeilles, or of Saint-Cyprien in the basin of the Dordogne with pronounced gorges both upstream at Beynac and downstream at Mouzens. Follow the Isle downstream from Périgueux and see how the valley broadens out in fertile basins each with its busy little town: Saint-Astier, Neuvic and Mussidan. Similar controls on settlement can be observed in the minor valleys, a clear illustration of which is to be found in the three valleys of the Dronne, Trincou and Côle which unite above Brantôme. Incised for the most part, these upper courses are not very attractive to settlement but where they do open out, there are villages: Quinsac on the Dronne, Villars on the Trincou, Saint-Pierre on the Côle.

Although in general the major rivers flow across the grain of the country, they do in places follow a geological boundary between hard and soft bands of rock and under these circumstances the opposing valley sides are likely to exhibit very different profiles. Such a situation is well illustrated by the Cingle de Trémolat on the Dordogne. Here one can stand on a cliff top immediately above the river on its north bank and look across the river to the gently sloping land within the great concave bend of the river to the south. This panoramic view is all the more impressive for the mosaic of land holdings and the richly varied land-use that can be seen within the meander loop. No one who has seen it can fail to understand the meaning of *polyculture.*

Where the river has cut down from one geological horizon to the next, a single cliff section is likely to show the effect of differential weathering and erosion. If hard rock overlies a softer one the result is usually an overhang, the more resistant limestone projecting above a cave-like hollow in the softer clays or marls beneath. Such features are often referred to as *abris* (shelters) since they were favoured as dwelling places by early man. They are most obvious in the gorge-like valley of the Vézère but are not uncommon elsewhere. Life in the abri cannot have been without its dangers from falling rocks, and broken bones have been found amongst the debris of the cave floors which suggest that not everyone was quick enough to escape a sudden death.

Undercutting of the cliffs is also brought about by the rivers, most commonly in their meandering sections where the current on the outside of the meander is directed against the cliff wall. The effect can be clearly seen in the Dronne valley near Bourdeilles and in that of the Vézère where the overhangs have created problems for road construction along the valley. Meanders seem to be developed best in the hard rocks and tend to occur in sequence rather than singly, but the relationship between meandering and the hardness of the rock into which they are incised is not necessarily a simple one, some authorities having suggested that the rivers have been superimposed on to the Cretaceous series from a cover of geologically younger rocks, now largely stripped away. Evidence in support of this theory is to be found in the sandy deposits which survive on the hilltops of the Sarladais and elsewhere and which still form a complete cover for the older rocks in the extreme west of the Dordogne region, in the Double, the Landais and the Bergeracois.

*Page 33*   Confluence of the Vézère and the Dordogne at Limeuil: well-cultivated valley plains contrasting with the wooded hills of Périgord Noir

*Page 34* (*above*) View in the Double; (*below*) houses in the *abri* at the Grotte du Grand Roc, Les Eyzies, showing typical roof lines and dormer windows

### THE DOUBLE AND THE LANDAIS

The *Double* is the name given to a small but distinctive *pays* in the extreme west of Périgord. Forested and lake-strewn it occupies the country between the Isle and Dronne rivers, its eastern limit being marked approximately by the line of the road from Mussidan to Ribérac (N709). The name is an ancient one—the Roman 'Edobula'—and although it has long been a forested region, the nature of the forest cover has changed over the course of time, pines having increasingly come to dominate the traditional deciduous woodland of oak, chestnut and hornbeam.

Between the Isle and the Dordogne is a very similar tract of country, the *Landais*, but here the name is a comparatively recent one and in general the forest cover is less complete than in the Double to the north. It comprises, in effect, an outlier of the great Landes forests to the south of Bordeaux, pine woods having been planted extensively in the early years of the present century when the resin-collecting industry was at its peak. The trees were tapped by collectors who moved to the area from the Landes and it is easy to see how the name came to be adopted. The eastern limit of the Landais is the Crempse valley, a small tributary valley of the Isle which is followed by the D38.

The acid and sometimes stony soils on which the forests of the Double and the Landais grow are derived from geologically youthful rocks of Tertiary (Oligocene) age. These are mainly sands, gravels and clays and are of continental origin, having been deposited by rivers draining the highlands of the Massif Central. They were laid down in what was then a basin of subsidence, some as almost level beds of sediment, others in the form of deltas or as irregular masses. Despite this variety of depositional forms, however, they share a general lack of resistance to erosion so that the two *pays* are characterised by

c

low hills with gentle, smoothed slopes. The relief may be described as indecisive. There is an overall absence of angularity and, with many small streams, the scenery is in sharp contrast with that of the limestone areas further east. The roundness of the slopes probably owes something also to the protection from heavy storms afforded by the vegetation cover, the roots of trees but more particularly the ground cover of ferns and heath plants. The visual effect of the forest is likewise to increase the impression of a flowing landscape.

There must be exceptions to a generalisation of this kind and in the Double and the Landais these are provided by bands of harder rock which cap the hills and also give rise to minor gorges and waterfalls in the valleys. The resistant bands have originated in one of two ways: either as layers of concretionary material which have been built up within the parent rocks, in a similar way to flints in chalk, or as a crust of iron-impregnated salts which has accumulated at the surface as a result of capillarity. Where these harder deposits form a capping to the hills they often preserve fragments of a former (Mio-Pliocene) erosion surface, this having a general height above sea-level of about 100 metres in the extreme west of the region, rising to around 150 metres in the east where calcareous rocks emerge from beneath the Tertiary cover. The planed summits are nowhere extensive enough, however, to interrupt the rounded lines of the landscape.

The smoothed outlines are not lost as a result of the downcutting of the tributary streams since their gorge like incisions are not apparent to the casual viewer. Yet on closer inspection these valleys with their youthful relief forms will be seen to provide a marked contrast to the mature hill slopes above them. They are not particularly deep, often no more than 25 metres, but they are steep-sided and narrow, miniatures almost of the gorges in the higher, eastern portion of Périgord, and their profiles owe much to the hard bands of rock referred to above. In section the latter create minor defiles and along the valley they give rise to small but highly picturesque water-falls.

Small lakes and marshes (*nauves*) are a common occurrence in the landscape hollows above the gorges, especially in the Double where they add greatly to the attractiveness of the scene since the forest has generally been cleared from their banks so that they are surrounded by open, grassy slopes. The lakes attract wildfowl, a useful addition to the scanty resources of the area and one which, with fish, complements the supply of game from the woods. Many of the lakes are now artificially controlled and they are used increasingly for recreation. They also provide drinking water for livestock, the Double, where it is not given over exclusively to forest, sharing the dairy and veal-producing interests of the Ribéracois to the north. Further south, in the Landais, the clearings in the forest are more likely to be devoted to vines and field crops or, increasingly, to orchard fruit.

The rivers flowing across the Tertiary rocks are less affected by them than are the minor streams. Nevertheless the valleys of the Isle below Mussidan and of the Dordogne below Bergerac are both broader and straighter than in the corresponding upstream sections. The concentration of life and activity in these valleys is in contrast with the sparsely populated environment of the Double and the Landais. To the south of the Dordogne, however, in the Bergeracois, there is a dense rural population that provides a striking exception to this difference between valley and watershed evident over such a large part of Périgord.

### THE BERGERACOIS

The Bergeracois has been described as the largest plain in Périgord, much of it being no more than 100 metres above sea-level. But the term is a misleading one if it implies that this part of the Dordogne region is flat, for the most striking charac-teristic of the local relief is its infinite variety. Indeed there is no

better word than 'sculptured' to describe the detailed nature of
the topography, the whole being a confused mosaic of finely
worked landforms. To the east, this landscape of the Bergeracois ends quite abruptly in the vicinity of Cadouin and Monpazier where the transition to older Cretaceous rocks is clear
from the increase in forest and a rapid thinning out of settlement.
Here is the *Pays de Belvès*, or *Pays de Bois*, where the limestones
are largely covered with lateritic ironstone or with Tertiary
sands and gravels.

The small-scale but very detailed relief of the Bergeracois
has come about as a result of the differential erosion of the
heterogeneous rocks of which this area is composed. They are
similar in age to those of the Double and the Landais but are of
different origin, having been built up as sediments in the shallow
seas and fringing lagoons of a once more extensive Bay of Biscay.
They have much in common, in fact, with the rocks of the
neighbouring Bordelais and Agenais which originated in the
same way and are best described as molasses with interbedded
bands of limestone. Sands and clays tend to predominate but
these are all calcareous to a greater or lesser degree. Beds of
much purer limestone are intercalated with the sands and clays,
however, and it is the differing resistance to erosion of these
contrasted rock bands that is responsible for the minute details
evident in the physical landscape.

Owing to the regional dip of the strata which is to the south-
west, the limestone bands tend to form eastward-facing escarpments but they are low and much fretted by erosion, Fénelon
describing them as *côtes démantelées*. The dip is not everywhere
uniform though and where the harder beds are more nearly
horizontal they often remain as cappings to knoll-like hills.
There are a large number of these in the vicinity of Issigeac
where the rock is a chalky white limestone and the district has
been called the *pays de tertres blancs*, literally the 'country of little
white knolls'. Elsewhere the presence of more resistant beds is
revealed in hillside benches and in the miniature gorges of

streams flowing to join the Dordogne or the Dropt. In places the outcrop of limestone is sufficiently extensive to give rise to karstic features such as dry valleys, for example near Faux. In contrast with the latter are landslip slopes typical where softer clays or sands predominate, the accumulation of mineral debris on the slopes probably having taken place as a result of the solifluction or mass-movement that took place when glacial conditions prevailed over northern Europe.

Tumuli which crown many hilltop sites are an indication of the long attraction which the Bergeracois has had for man. The complexity of the landforms is mirrored in a variety of soils and local climates which has offered a wide range of opportunities to the farmer. Vines (Monbazillac) and plums flourish as they do further to the south and west, but many field crops are also grown and there are patches of woodland or scrub on the sandier outcrops. The alternation of rock bands means that a water supply is easily obtained from springs or wells, and windmills once crowned the more exposed hilltops. Certain of the larger hills have also provided defensive sites for fortified towns like Beaumont-du-Périgord that was built during the long struggles between the English and French crowns for possession of this territory. These wars as they affected Périgord are treated more fully in the chapter which follows.

# 3    CAPITAL OF PREHISTORY

ON 12 September 1940, near the small town of Montignac in the valley of the Vézère, a boy's dog disappeared down a hole left by an uprooted tree. The
boy, called Ravidat, and his companions widened the hole in
order to retrieve the dog and literally fell into what has become
probably the world's most famous cave, the great Hall of Bulls
at Lascaux. The story is almost as well known as the cave, and
it is interesting to note how prominently boys feature in this
kind of discovery. Almost half a century earlier, in 1895, a
group of them first observed the engravings on the walls of the
cave at La Mouthe near Les Eyzies and it was this earlier discovery, following the one at Altamira in northern Spain, that
confirmed the authenticity of Palaeolithic cave art.

The Dordogne region has a special significance for anyone
interested in the history of man. In addition to the caves with
their wall paintings, engravings and sculptures, there are a
great many rock shelters (*abris*), the accumulated debris of
which (*gisements*) has yielded an enormous amount of evidence
about early man, his way of life and culture. Over 200 gisements have been investigated in Périgord and of these more
than half are in the valley of the river Vézère, many of them
near to the village of Les Eyzies which deserves its title of
'Capital of Prehistory'. Several of the abris can now be visited
and the results of the archaeological investigations observed *in
situ*. The caves likewise can be seen, though unhappily not
Lascaux which is closed except to a very few selected visitors.
There are also a number of museums where archaeological finds

40

are on display. Of these the best local one is the rather grandly titled *Musée Nationale de Préhistoire* at Les Eyzies, housed in a medieval château which was itself built on an abri level. Another is the so-called *maison-forte* (fortified house or small castle) at Reignac higher up the valley, where attempts have been made to reconstruct scenes of life in the abris. Near Thonac a newly opened centre (1973) has exhibits illustrating the range and skills of prehistoric art. Mention must also be made of the excellent *Musée du Périgord* in Périgueux which in France is second only to Saint-Germain-en-Laye near Paris as a museum of prehistory. For fuller details of all these places to visit, the reader is advised to consult the latest edition of the *Michelin Green Guide*.

## LES EYZIES

What were the advantages of the lower Vézère valley that made it so attractive to early man? Accessibility must be regarded as one of these, although the Vézère was no more accessible than certain other valleys like that of the Isle, the convergence of routes upon which has already been emphasised. As a whole, however, the valleys of Périgord lay astride routes from Mediterranean Europe to the north as well as from east to west, so that prehistoric man would pass through the area in the course of his migrations and would observe its other attractions.

Amongst these a factor of major importance was the cover and defence afforded by the abris, natural shelters with their overhanging rock ceilings. Since they were some way up the valley side they provided an ideal retreat from the dangers of wild animals or enemies and, with a fire burning, their inner recesses offered protection from the severe cold of winter. They may not have been continuously occupied throughout the year; during the summer months they were probably abandoned as the hunters pursued the reindeer and other sources of food, and the remains of what appear to have been summer camps have

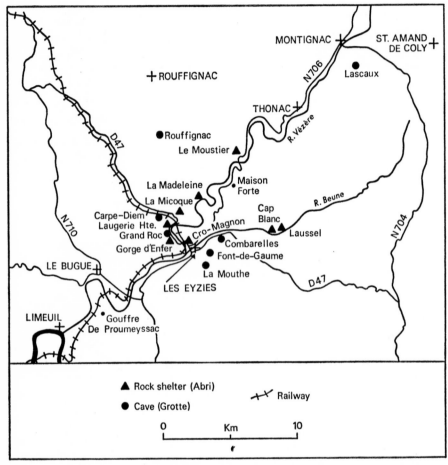

Fig 3  Archaeological sites of the Vézère valley

been investigated in other parts of Périgord at Rabier, near Bergerac, and at Solvieux, near Mussidan. With the onset of winter, however, the abri would be inhabited again and, allowing for this kind of temporary use, some of them appear to have had almost continuous occupation from prehistoric times to the present day. Houses are still to be seen, both in the Vézère valley and elsewhere, built into the rock shelters and using the natural features as far as possible to provide both the back wall and a part of the roof. Inevitably man has added to the work of nature, hollowing out the shelters in places and even making 'windows' in the rock face. This has happened when families have been forced to seek refuge in time of war and an example of work that dates from the Hundred Years War can be seen at the Roc de Tayac on the valley side opposite the village of Tayac near Les Eyzies. Evidence can also be seen of the channels cut in the cliff above the dwellings to prevent water draining into the houses from above.

The lower Vézère valley is particularly well endowed with rock shelters owing to the nature of the local limestone which is here massive and jointed, less friable or crumbly for example than that of the nearby Dordogne valley. Another attraction lay in the gorge-like constrictions of the valley where hunted animals could fairly easily be trapped by making barriers. Animals were also pursued on the plateaux above and they could be stampeded over the cliffs where they fell to their death below. Flint, from which weapons and tools were made, was available not only from the plateau tops but also from the river gravels in the valleys, and the animals that were caught yielded bone and horn as well as skins, fur and wool for clothing and other domestic uses. Amongst the weapons made were harpoons, used to catch fish which supplemented the diet of meat and whatever berries and edible plants could be gathered in the generally tundra-like climatic conditions.

Archaeological investigation of the gisements in the Vézère valley and elsewhere has revealed evidence of human occupation that goes back to the Lower Palaeolithic although the 'golden age' of prehistory in Périgord was undoubtedly the later, Upper Palaeolithic—the age of the cave paintings as well as of very sophisticated tools and personal ornaments.

The oldest finds have come from the gisement at La Micoque where flint tools, neatly worked on two faces, date from the Acheulian period of the Lower Palaeolithic making them up to half a million years old. Of much greater interest than these, however, are the skeletal remains of primitive man which have been discovered at a number of sites and which belong to the Middle Palaeolithic or Mousterian. Indeed this latter period derives its name from the remains of Neanderthal man found in a rock shelter above the village of Le Moustier in 1909. Other finds of a similar kind were made about the same time at La Ferrassie which is near Savignac-de-Miremont in the Manaurie valley—a tributary of the Vézère—and much later in 1957, at Regourdon near Lascaux. From the discoveries in these places it is possible to build up a picture of Neanderthal man which shows him to have been short—about 1·55 metres—but sturdy with long, well-muscled arms. His head was long, with a receding forehead but prominent brows and teeth that projected from a snout-like jaw. His flint tools were more finely worked and pointed than those of his predecessors, of necessity perhaps since the climatic conditions under which he lived gradually worsened with the onset of the last phase of the Ice Age, and he was compelled to turn from a mainly vegetarian way of life to hunting.

Very different from this primitive race of man were the first examples of *Homo sapiens* who seem to have reached this part of France some 40,000 years ago at the beginning of what has come to be distinguished as the Upper Palaeolithic. He was like modern man, upright and with a large cranial capacity, indicative of his bigger brain, and it was this man who was responsible for the cave paintings and the finely worked tools and personal ornaments found in the rock shelters. There were two distinct racial types of *Homo Sapiens* living in Périgord during the Upper Palaeolithic. In the museum at Périgord is a skeleton found at nearby Chancelade in 1888 and this man was short with prominent cheekbones not unlike the modern Eskimo. He was a hunter of reindeer and moved northwards following the reindeer herds at the close of the Palaeolithic when the climate became warmer. Chancelade man would have looked strikingly different from Cro-Magnon man whose appearance in the region came somewhat earlier. He was much taller—1·80 to 1·90 metres—with long, muscular limbs and he derives his name from the rock shelter close to Les Eyzies where three skeletons were unearthed in 1868. They were found during work on the railway embankment and the abri is still there, though a mental reconstruction of the scene is not made easier by the fact that it serves as the garage of the Cro-Magnon hotel. Anthropologists contend that characteristics of Cro-Magnon man are to be seen in the population of Périgord at the present day.

*Divisions of French Prehistory*

| | |
|---|---|
| Iron Age | 750 BC |
| Bronze Age | 1650 BC |
| Neolithic | 3000 BC |
| Mesolithic | 10000 BC |
| Upper Palaeolithic { | Magdalenian |
| | Solutrean |
| | Aurignacian |
| Middle Palaeolithic or Mousterian | |
| Lower Palaeolithic | |

The 1860s were formative years in the archaeological world as a succession of major discoveries were made in this small portion of the valley around Les Eyzies and it is impossible to explore the area at the present day without feeling a sense of the excitement that there must have been as these major new finds were made. Despite the incongruities introduced by the tourist

45

industry such as the statue of Neanderthal man standing sentinel over the museum at Les Eyzies, there is always the feeling that new discoveries are to be made. After all, Lascaux was unknown little more than thirty years ago.

It was Edouard Lartet, a French archaeologist and his English friend, Henry Christy, who were responsible for the first scientific excavations made in the 1860s. They studied systematically the gisements at Laugerie, Le Moustier, La Madeleine and elsewhere, and on the basis of their finds were able to establish an accurate chronology of French prehistory. They gave the names of several of these rock shelters to the time divisions which they recognised, Magdalenian for example being that given to the final period of the Upper Palaeolithic. By this last phase, weapons and tools had achieved a high degree of sophistication and finely worked arrow and spear heads could be made by skilful pressure of flint on flint rather than simply by the older methods of flaking. Bone, horn and ivory were used to manufacture objects which included harpoons and needles, scrapers and blades, and many of these objects can be examined in the museums at Les Eyzies and Périgueux.

Some of the abris have yielded examples of engraving and rock sculpture as well as human remains and artifacts, though unhappily few have been allowed to remain *in situ*. An exception is the remarkable engraving of a salmon that was found on the roof of a rock shelter in the Gorge d'Enfer in 1912. It is doubly interesting, firstly because representations of fish are rare and secondly, for quite a different reason, because it was actually sold to a German museum by the local mayor soon after its discovery, and although the sale was prevented by the Department of Fine Arts it was not before deep incisions had been made into the rock above and below the sculpture, preparatory to removing it. Less fortunate was the 'Venus of Laussel', the engraved figure of a naked woman that was found at Laussel beneath a vast overhanging rock which towers above

Fig 4   A sketch of Les Eyzies in the 1860s (from an original in Lartet and Christy's *Reliquiae Aquitanicae*)

the valley of the Beune, but was removed by Dr Lalanne, its discoverer. It is well known to archaeologists and is thought to have been some kind of fertility symbol making up part of a shrine. There is a model of it in the museum at Les Eyzies. Although there is nothing to see now at Laussel, the nearby Abri de Cap Blanc is well worth a visit for its group of sculptured animals. They are mainly of horses but include what are probably two bison. Carvings of this kind tell one what animals were hunted in Périgord ten to forty thousand years ago. Still better evidence, however, comes from the paintings and engravings that are to be seen on the walls of certain caves.

To avoid disappointment it is worth remembering that not all the caves that can be visited in the vicinity of Les Eyzies yield examples of cave art. Two of them, the Grotte du Grand Roc and the Grotte de Carpe Diem at Manaurie, are famous for their natural formations, stalactites, stalagmites and crystal formations, and are worth seeing for the sake of these, especially the former. In order to look at paintings and engravings it is necessary to visit three caves in the hillside to the south of the village, all within a couple of kilometres of each other: the Grotte de la Mouthe, the Grotte de Font-de-Gaume and the Grotte des Combarelles. The first of these was discovered accidentally in 1895, the others a few years later after the remarkable finds at La Mouthe had led to renewed archaeological interest in the area. A fourth cave, the Grotte de Rouffignac, was discovered much more recently in 1956. This is about 15 kilometres north of Les Eyzies but worth the journey by picturesque, winding country roads.

The figures represented in the caves are mostly animals but these include many different kinds: reindeer, bison, oxen, horses, ibex or wild goat, stags, woolly rhinoceroses, mammoths (for which Rouffignac is specially noted), bears, lions, hyenas and wolves. It is a stylised art, partly abstract; the animals are generally single figures seen from the side, but occasionally arranged in groups. They are not shown against any kind of landscape background, yet they are far from being lifeless figures. Indeed many of them seem to have been frozen in the act of leaping, running, falling, even swimming, so that the impression they convey is one of activity and movement. In some cases the natural features of the rock face have been cleverly exploited to heighten this impression and seen in the flickering light of a 'roman' lamp the animals must almost have come alive. Drawings of spears or arrows superimposed on the bodies of the animals suggest that the purpose behind their representation was to ensure success in hunting. Men painted the beast they wished to capture and so put it in their power. Such a functional explanation is borne out by the fact that the decorated portions of the caves are well away from the inhabited rock shelters, some distance into the hillside, and one can only speculate about the magical rites that took place in these remote caverns. Certainly this was not art for its own sake; the pictures had a real part to play in relation to man's survival.

Human figures are less common than those of animals and the representation of faces is rare. When they are present the figures often appear to be masked. Perhaps they were the priests or magic men who officiated at the ceremonial rites. Impressions of human hands are sometimes to be found. The latter are thought to be an early form of cave art—what more natural, given some colour and a blank surface, than to draw round one's fingers. In addition to the human and animal forms, the cave decorations also include some inanimate forms. They are usually little more than symbols and are known to archaeologists as *tectiforms*. Their purpose is uncertain. They may have been artists' marks or signs which denoted the tribal group or groups who made use of the cave for their magical ceremonies. Alternatively they could be a crude attempt to portray the rough shelters that were built by the huntsmen in the summer.

Apart from a little rock sculpture, the technique of decoration was either engraving or painting. The Grotte de Font-de-Gaume should be visited for the best examples of the latter and

49

the Grotte des Combarelles, where there are between 300 and 400 engraved figures, for the former. Some of the paintings are monochromes, usually in black, but others are finely coloured in shades of red, brown and yellow. The colours were derived from mineral ochres which would be powdered and mixed with fat before being applied to the wall of the cave, probably using some kind of plant stem.

## LASCAUX

Lascaux has been called the 'Sistine of Prehistory' so remarkable is the quality of its paintings. They have been preserved in such an excellent state because of their distance from the original entrance to the cave which protected them from changes of weather and climate, and because of a natural varnish they have somehow acquired in the form of a very fine coating of crystalline calcite. It is all the more tragic therefore that the public should no longer be able to see them. Fortunately, however, there are photographs, and soon it will be possible to visit a reconstruction of the cave with copies of the animals in their correct position on the walls, coloured for the most part with natural pigments.

When Lascaux was opened to the public after World War II the entrance was an artificial one, access being almost directly into the Hall of Bulls. No longer were the paintings insulated from changes in the weather and they were also exposed to the artificial atmosphere created by the breathing of up to 2,000 visitors a day. By the early 1950s experts had begun to suspect that the paintings were suffering from the newly created environment but it was another ten years before the danger was sufficiently appreciated for the cave to be closed. The paintings had been affected by what came to be known as 'green sickness' (*mal vert*) and 'white sickness' (*mal blanc*), the former being due to the growth of a minute plant organism, the latter to a coating of calcite which appeared as a second stage

*Page 51*    (*above*) Rock sculpture, now in the museum at Les Eyzies; (*below*) painting
of a horse in the Lascaux cave

*Page 52*
Reconstruction of Lascaux: Hi Se Lee, the Korean painter, working on a study of two bulls

in the process of deterioration. The figure of a horse had been most seriously harmed, but now the temperature, humidity and chemical composition of the atmosphere in the cave is strictly controlled and the process of deterioration is believed to have been checked. A scientific commission has studied the problem and has recommended that five people a day may now be permitted to visit the cave, for a period not exceeding 20 minutes, but there is little possibility of the general public being allowed to enter in the foreseeable future. The facsimile steel and concrete cave, which is being created with absolute attention to detail and is only a short distance from the original, will be some compensation.

### CIVITAS PETROCORIORUM

After about 10,000 BC the climate began to get warmer as the northern ice sheets melted. The tundra-like conditions of the Palaeolithic gave way gradually to forest; the reindeer-hunters moved northwards following their quarry and with these changes came an end to the culture represented by Lascaux, Font-de-Gaume and other sites. To the people who remained— the hunters of the Mesolithic—the rock shelters were less essential as a retreat from the cold. Instead they built wooden shelters, often close to the river where they could fish and catch beaver. Snails seem to have featured prominently in their diet although there were still plenty of animals to be caught in the woods. The cave at Rouffignac has yielded a variety of tools of the period, including pointed objects that might have been used as fishing hooks, but these are a mundane legacy compared with the art of the Palaeolithic.

Agriculture and pastoralism were introduced to the Dordogne region in the third millennium BC and clearings were made in the forests by these early farmers. They made use of highly polished stone tools and had pottery, but the most striking contribution to the landscape of the Neolithic peoples lies in the

D

stone monuments which they erected—megaliths. They were the first great builders. Périgord, though, is not the place to visit if one wishes to study the finest examples of the new art. There are a few dolmen, massive stones which formed part of a burial chamber—there is a good example at Brantôme—but there are none of the extraordinary monuments that one sees along the Atlantic coast and, above all, in Brittany. The Neolithic in Périgord is of some interest, however, in pointing to the growing importance of the river valleys as routeways. From discoveries of stone implements it is clear that the valley of the Isle in particular was assuming the role that was to grow in succeeding centuries, making it the focus of regional life.

With the adoption of metal, first bronze from about 1650 BC, and later iron, the demand for new materials meant that the valleys were used increasingly for trade. Tin was brought from Brittany en route for the Mediterranean, as well as copper and gold, and implements made from these metals have been unearthed in burial mounds. The richest finds in Périgord came from a tomb at Singleyrac in the Bergeracois and there are many other tumuli in the same locality. With the exception of this one area, however, the region as a whole remained sparsely populated with none of the importance of, say, Médoc or Vendée at this time.

But change was to come with the substitution of iron. Introduced by Celtic-speaking peoples, refugees from central Europe, the adoption of this metal resulted in the region emerging from a long period of relative obscurity that can be said to have begun with the collapse of the Palaeolithic cave-art culture. The reason lay in the presence of easily accessible iron ores. They occurred in nodular form in the sandy deposits which cap many of the hills of Périgord (page 25) and could be obtained simply by digging holes at the surface. Another advantage was the extensive forest cover that provided an abundant supply of charcoal for treating the ores. So plentiful were the raw materials that Périgord became famous for the quality of its iron and it was exported widely to other parts of Europe, especially to the emerging cities of the Mediterranean world. The local population grew in response to the prosperity that came with the iron industry and it has been supposed that the total population may have been as large as 200,000 by the time of the Roman conquest in 56 BC. Any such estimate must be treated with considerable caution—the population of the département of Dordogne at the present day totals only 380,000—yet despite uncertainty over actual numbers, there is no doubt that the centuries preceding Roman invasion were prosperous ones and that some kind of organised society had emerged in the Dordogne region which looked to the middle Isle valley as the focus of its administrative life. Within this territory were four tribes—the Petrocorii—loosely federated and ruled from a single capital, Vesunna.

The situation of Vesunna was ideal from the point of view of access to all parts of the tribal territory. It was also well sited for defence, occupying two steep-sided hills which rise sharply above the southern bank of the Isle. Between them is a small tributary valley, that of the Campniac, where springs (the *Fos Vesunna*) afforded a plentiful supply of water. To this fortress and tribal centre would come travellers and traders from other parts of western Europe and from them was acquired knowledge of the wealth and might of the emergent Roman Empire to the south. There was much to be envied in the Roman way of life, not least their wines, and that may help to explain the relative ease with which Périgord and the rest of south-western France was brought under Roman rule following the invasion of 56 BC. After conquest the land of the Petrocorii became absorbed in one of three divisions of Aquitania which extended between them from the Loire to the Pyrenees, but the native population prospered under Roman domination and a sense of the old territorial unit was never lost.

One has to be a very unobservant traveller in Périgord not to recognise the many place-names that end in the suffix *-ac*:

55

Ribérac, Montignac, Salignac and hundreds more. They are as common as the place-names ending in *-ham* or *-ton* in the English Midlands and have much the same origin, meaning simply 'the place' or 'the holding' of a particular family or group. They are Roman names, derived from *agus*, and may indicate the Gallo-Roman origin of the settlement although it is likely that some of the older Gaulish (Celtic) settlements also adopted the Roman usage. It would be surprising indeed if this did not happen since the native population gradually adopted the Latin language. In turn the latter developed into the southern form of French known as the *langue d'oc*.

In terms of building the legacy of Rome is much less obvious than it is with regard to place-names. Sites of villas can be investigated but the most visible monuments to Roman civilisation are to be seen in Périgueux itself which continued to grow and to exercise its administrative role. Under Roman rule the well-defended but rather inconvenient site on the hills south of the river was abandoned, and a new settlement of Vésone built on the more gently sloping north bank within the broad curve of the river. It became a flourishing and lively regional capital from which roads radiated outwards to the other important Roman towns; north to Limoges, north-west to Saintes, south-west to Bordeaux and to Agen, south-east to Cahors and beyond towards Lyon, capital of Roman Gaul. Public buildings included an amphitheatre, baths and a temple which also served as a general meeting place. The central portion of this temple, the *Tour de Vésone*, is still there, as are the ruins of the amphitheatre, now in the more peaceful setting of a public garden (page 184).

Vésone enjoyed three centuries of peace and progress until, in the year AD 276, it suffered invasion by 'barbarians' (*Alamans*) from the north, forerunners of those other, bigger groups who were to follow after the collapse of Roman administration. Many of the fine buildings were destroyed and the sense of security lost, so that after the invasion the rebuilt town was enclosed within a wall. Stones from the ruins were used in constructing the wall and in the fragments that still remain it is possible to see carved stones that once had a more distinguished role to play in the decoration of some public building or dwelling. The name *Civitas Petrocoriorum* was given to the rebuilt town and the portion of Périgueux that corresponds with the Roman settlement is still known as *La Cité*.

## DARK AGES

The third century, which saw the first invasion of barbarians, also witnessed the gradual spread of Christianity and the coincidence of these two events was of great significance, the Church providing the one force capable of maintaining the region's identity during the centuries of war and disorder that were to follow. When the diocese of Périgueux was defined in the mid-fourth century its boundaries were based closely on the area already administered by the Roman *Cité*, and the subsequent organisation of the diocese owed much to its inheritance of the Roman administrative tradition. The first bishop, Paternus, was appointed in the year 365.

Peace which had been restored during the final century of Roman rule was again destroyed at the beginning of the fifth century with the eruption of the Vandals from central Europe. They passed through Aquitaine on their way to Spain or North Africa leaving a trail of destruction and were followed almost at once by the Goths. These latter people, originating probably from much the same part of northern Europe as the Angles, Saxons and Jutes who were soon to invade Britain, had followed a long migratory route that had taken them through much of the civilised Mediterranean world. Although they had sacked Rome in AD 410, they had picked up some of the cultural traits of the peoples they had conquered so that the rule which they subsequently established over the whole of Aquitaine, including Périgord, was not wholly repressive despite their opposition to the Christian Church. Visigoth (ie Western Goth) control of Aquitaine lasted for almost a century, ending in 507 after the victory of the Franks under Clovis at the battle of Vouillé near Poitiers. The Franks, who had established a 'French' kingdom north of the Loire, now extended their rule over most of the south, displacing the Goths, and the term *Merovingian* is applied to the succession of kings who followed Clovis.

Merovingian rule was affected by family squabbles which resulted in division and redivision of territory, but for the rural population of Périgord and the remainder of Aquitaine the changes were of little concern. Politically, however, they were weakening and left the country once again vulnerable to invasion. Gascons (or *Vascones*), descended it is thought from a population who had earlier taken refuge in the Pyrenees, came and settled south of the Garonne in that portion of the southwest which subsequently came to be known as Gascony. The name *Guyenne*, thought to be a corruption of *Aquitaine* was later applied to lands north of the Garonne which included Périgord. But the most disastrous consequences of weak rule came with the brief but destructive incursion of Arabs from Spain. They swept rapidly north until they were defeated by Charles Martel, again near Poitiers, in AD 732. Their retreat was equally fast and probably still more damaging of property, but the whole episode has managed to acquire so much Arthurian-type legend over the years that it is difficult to separate fact from fiction. Amongst outrages committed in Périgord was the pillaging of the monastic settlement at Calviac on the Dordogne above Domme.

Charles Martel was the founder of a new line of Frankish kings, the Carolingians, and after the withdrawal of the Arabs a long struggle took place between the Carolingian leaders and local rulers for control of the south-west. Local resistance eventually collapsed with the defeat of the Gascon leader, Waïfre, at Périgueux in 768 and his subsequent assassination. To consolidate his hold over this part of his dominion, Charles the

Great—Charlemagne—installed one of his vassals, Wisbode, as Count of Périgord and it was this man who founded the abbey at Brantôme in 779. Périgord was a part of the newly created kingdom of Aquitaine, itself a division of the Empire, and the count and his successors built their castles in Périgueux and at Montignac in the valley of the Vézère—known for a long time as Montignac-le-Comte.

During the ninth century a new threat appeared in the form of the Vikings who followed the coast and then used their longboats to move up the rivers, pillaging settlements and massacring those of their inhabitants caught unawares or foolhardy enough to resist rather than seeking safety in the forest. Périgord was not spared these raids despite its inland position and by the 840s the 'pirates' were reaching as far upriver as Périgueux. Following the Isle, a band of them destroyed the settlements at Montpon and Mussidan in 849 and then attacked Périgueux itself, burning the part of the town not protected by its walls. The latter included Puy Saint-Front, a monastic suburb that had grown up around the tomb of the apostle who, it was supposed, had brought Christianity to Périgord. Other attacks followed in 853 and 865, and in a vain attempt to protect his town the bishop had forts built lower down the valley at Saint-Astier and upstream at Bassillac. But little could deter the raiders, and at Moustier in the Vézère valley there are traces of a canal they are said to have made in order to keep out of range of rocks hurled down at them from the Roque-Saint-Christophe on the opposite bank. Terrasson was sacked so the canal must have served its purpose. Eventually, however, the Périgordins found a leader in Wlgrin, the king's brother-in-law, who fought successfully against the invaders and was rewarded with the name *Taillefer* (literally, sword of iron, and later Talleyrand) and by being made Count of Périgord.

Despite all their political upheavals, five centuries of invasion had not greatly changed the way of life of the native population in Périgord, who continued to cultivate the more favoured

59

valleys and retreated to the forest clearings in times of stress. Numerically the impact of the newcomers was not great. They had come to plunder or to rule, and local customs and the Latin language were only gradually modified by their presence. Furthermore, the role of the Church ensured that a sense of territorial unity survived amongst the descendants of the Petrocorii.

TROUBADOURS AND BASTIDES

Successive counts of Périgord were less successful than the Church in maintaining unity. Their authority was often weak, power at the local level being exercised by barons or *seigneurs*. There were four baronies—Beynac, Biron, Bourdeilles and Mareuil—and rivalry between them was so intense that they were usually referred to collectively in order that no one of them should appear to have precedence over the others. The barons, and also local lords, built castles for defence and to enhance their reputations—these were the places to which the population looked for protection when skirmishing broke out between rival leaders. Struggles of this kind were a constant occurrence in the early Middle Ages and the overall power of the count had been so reduced by the eleventh century that Nontron and the plateau country in the north-east had passed under the control of the *vicomté* of Limoges, whilst the lords of Bergerac looked for leadership to Bordeaux rather than to Périgueux.

But there was a creative side to medieval feuding and this had its expression in the lyric poetry of the troubadours which flourished in Périgord and neighbouring parts of the south-west during the twelfth and thirteenth centuries. Written in the *langue d'oc*, the language that had evolved in the south, the songs told of courtly love, battles and of the human weaknesses that were revealed in those troubled times. Young warriors would sing of their feats in love and war—both real and imaginary— and they soon became so popular that it was claimed 'the entire South sang'. Most famous of the love poets was Arnaud

60

Daniel of Ribérac whom Dante described as 'he who surpasses all other poets of his land by songs of love and narratives of romance'.

A very different personality was Bertrand de Born, lord of Hautefort, who wrote 'sonnets in coats of mail'. Bertrand typified the fiercely independent noblemen of his time, fighting his brother Constantin for possession of the family seat at Hautefort. For this struggle he enlisted the help of Henry Court-Mantel, the rebellious son of Henry II, whilst Constantin was supported by Court-Mantel's brother, Richard Coeur de Lion. Bertrand is said to have hurled verses at his enemies as though they were blows from his sword and 'the din of battle and the passion of hatred make themselves felt all through his fierce and unbridled verses' (Emile Faguet). Little wonder that Dante confined him to his 'Inferno'.

To appreciate the context in which Bertrand's battles were fought it is necessary to look back to the middle of the eleventh century when a new and powerful Duchy of Aquitaine was established under the leadership of the Count of Poitou. The duchy flourished for some eighty years virtually independent of the French crown, but in 1137 the two were united by the marriage of Eleanor, daughter of Duke Guillaume X who had no male heir, to the future King Louis VII. In spite of her marriage, however, Eleanor ensured that the duchy retained a large measure of independence and in 1152 she divorced her husband and three weeks later married the future King of England, Henry Plantagenet, Count of Anjou and Duke of Normandy. When Henry was crowned Henry II in 1154 he joined most of western France to the English crown. The rise of his rival was viewed, understandably, with some fear by Louis and the seeds of future conflict between the two crowns were sown. The struggle was to be most protracted in Aquitaine, lasting for three centuries during which local barons such as Bertrand de Born lost few opportunities of exploiting the situation for their own gain.

To help control his Empire, Henry appointed his sons as viceroys and Richard was given charge of Aquitaine. But they had little authority and at various times rebelled against their father, usually with the support of their mother. Richard's task was particularly difficult. He was opposed by local rulers, including the Count of Périgord, and also by his eldest brother, Henry, who tried to wrest Aquitaine from him but died at Martel (in Quercy) in 1183, supposedly in an agony of conscience after pillaging the shrine at Rocamadour. Richard succeeded his father as king and duke in 1189, but Aquitaine, like England, saw little of him, his energies being devoted to crusading in the Holy Land. Yet he died in Aquitaine, killed by an arrow besieging the castle of a rebellious baron at Chalus (Limousin) in 1199. He was succeeded in turn as king-duke by his brother John whose reign was marked in Aquitaine by the Albigensian crusade when cruel persecution took place of those who professed the new doctrine of Catharism. The heresy had spread to Périgord where religion became yet another excuse for violence and assault. Houses were burnt, crops destroyed and the rock shelter and cave once more became a place of refuge.

Périgueux emerged during the twelfth century as a dual town, the rivalry between its two halves symbolising the divisions of the time. The Cité was the residence of the count and his followers and the cathedral of Saint-Etienne was the focus of the religious life of the diocese. Here was traditional authority. But only a short distance away, on rising ground in the east, was the rebuilt settlement of Puy Saint-Front where merchants and craftsmen congregated. They represented the emancipated bourgeoisie, intolerant of feudal government. By 1183 the upstart settlement was sufficiently strong and free to be granted its own seal, and municipal independence from the Cité was symbolised by a separate town wall. For protection against the count the citizens looked to the king, but to the King of France rather than of England, and in 1204 Philip

Augustus rewarded their loyalty with the grant of certain royal privileges. Encouraged, they reached an agreement with their fellow citizens in the Cité in 1240 to unite the two towns under a common council. Opposition from the count prevented this coming into force until 1251 when royal authority again intervened. After that the twin towns were effectively one, but the old division is still evident in the layout of Périgueux at the present time (page 185).

Despite the troubled nature of the times, the early Middle Ages were marked by a growth of population and gradual clearance of forest for agriculture. In this the Church was a formative influence. New parishes were created, frequently adding the names of saints, and *sauvetés* were founded. The latter were planned villages which enjoyed the special protection of the Church, crosses indicating the boundary of the village lands. There are several in the more wooded parts of Périgord, recognisable by names such as *La Sauvetat* or *La Salvetat*.

Religious orders also played a part in developing the land, establishing their monasteries or convents in some of the least accessible places. Périgord Noir was especially favoured because of its protecting forests, though the monastic buildings were often fortified as well to guard the treasures from pillage and theft. The abbey church of the Augustinians at Saint-Amand-de-Coly near Lascaux is a particularly fine example with its castle-like entrance and other defensive works. Of the Cistercian foundations the best known is that of Cadouin in the Forêt de la Bessède, south of the great loops of the Dordogne. It became a place of pilgrimage after it acquired a piece of linen believed to be part of the Holy Shroud and at the end of the fifteenth century the abbey was enriched by the addition of an elaborately decorated Gothic cloister. The religious orders differed widely in the extent of their withdrawal from the world or their involvement with it and its problems. Even the most retiring tended to attract settlement to their monasteries because of their need of food and service. In the town they acted as a still greater catalyst to growth and the example of Saint-Front at Périgueux has been cited. Pilgrims came here too, visiting the apostle's tomb on their way to Compostela. At Sarlat the romanesque tower of Saint-Sacerdos is a reminder of the monastic settlement which first drew people to what was a naturally inaccessible spot. Terrasson likewise benefited from its monastery of Saint-Sour.

It is evident from the sauvetés and other religious foundations that the spread of settlement in the Middle Ages was far from being a wholly random process. Still more convincing proof of this is to be found in the *bastides* (from *bâtir*, to build), planned towns that were built, for the most part, during the second half of the thirteenth century and the early years of the fourteenth. Town foundation was a profitable source of investment to the medieval landowner who, in return for the granting of privileges to the newly settled burgesses, was able to draw revenues from the town in the form of rents and market tolls. He was also assured of the support of the townspeople in time of war. To the population the new town offered a welcome measure of freedom from feudal authority—many took the name of *Villefranche*—and the walls gave protection.

According to Professor Beresford, in his book *New Towns of the Middle Ages* (1967), the expanding wine trade acted as a stimulus to town plantation in Aquitaine during the thirteenth century, and Périgord lay on the northern edge of the colonisation zone. At least twenty new towns were founded in Périgord, though the evidence for some of them is only documentary and others are very decayed or reduced to a handful of farmhouses. Most are in the south, along the Dordogne which acted as an outlet for the wine, and in the Bergeracois where soils are fertile and good defensive sites were provided by low hills rising sharply from the plain. But a number of towns were founded further north, Beauregard in the forested country between the Dordogne and the Isle, and Saint-Barthélemy-de-Bellegarde in the Double. These latter settlements provide excellent examples of forest colonisation and their cultivated fields are still surrounded by woodland even today. Monpazier, south of the Dordogne, similarly gives the impression of being set in a large forest clearing.

Edward, son of the English King Henry III, was made Duke of Aquitaine by his father in 1254 and many of the bastides were founded during his reign as duke or king (1272–1307). They were generally established in partnership with a local landowner, the king's agent acting for him at this stage and again later when taxes and tolls had to be collected. A smaller number were founded by the French in those portions of Périgord which owed allegiance to the King of France or to the Count of Toulouse. Domme, for example, was established by the King of France in 1281 soon after the Treaty of Amiens had ceded territories in Aquitaine to Edward (including the new town of Eymet, an earlier French foundation). Domme came under English rule in 1310 but was lost and regained several times before it finally passed under French control towards the end of the Hundred Years' War. The south of Périgord was very much a frontier territory at this time and the political and defensive role of the new towns was at times as important as the economic one. To cross from the south to the north bank of the Dordogne was 'to go to France'.

Defence considerations meant that hilltop sites were preferred for the new towns. Domme is the classic example, built on a crag which towers hundreds of feet above the Dordogne, presenting an almost sheer face to the north. On the other sides it is protected by deeply cut tributary valleys around which the modern road winds in a series of sharp bends. The journey is worthwhile, for Domme has been attractively restored in recent years and the panoramic views from the cliff top over the valley and hills of Périgord Noir beyond are unrivalled except perhaps by those from the castles at Beynac or Castelnaud. Beaumont-du-Périgord (1272)—with Domme and Monpazier the most complete of the bastides—also has a hilltop site as its

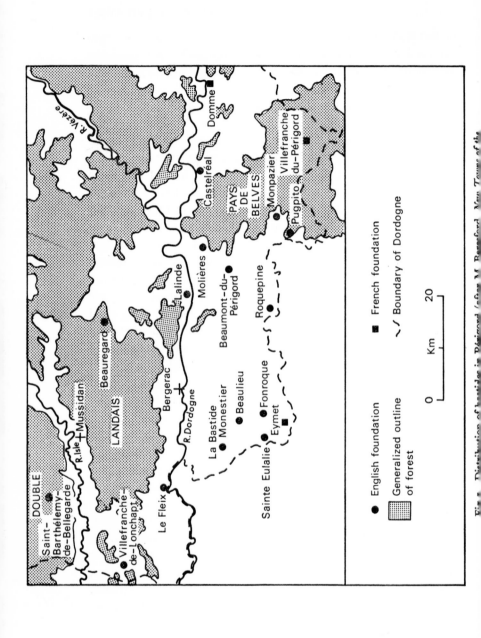

Fig 4. Distribution of bastides in Périgord (after M. Beresford, *New Towns of the*

**Legend:**

● English foundation

■ French foundation

▨ Generalized outline of forest

⌇ Boundary of Dordogne

0    20
|————————|
Km

**Labelled places and features:**

DOUBLE

Saint-Barthélemy-de-Bellegarde

R. Isle — Mussidan

LANDAIS

Beauregard

Villefranche-de-Lonchapt

Le Fleix

Bergerac

R. Dordogne

La Bastide Monestier

Beaulieu

Sainte Eulalie

Fonroque

Eymet

Roquepine

Beaumont-du-Périgord

Molières

Lalinde

Castelréal

Domme

PAYS DE BELVES

Monpazier

Villefranche-du-Périgord

Pugpito-du-Périgord

R. Vézère

name suggests. Names descriptive of the site were often given to the newly planted towns; witness Beaulieu and Beauregard. Other good examples of hilltop settlements are Saint-Barthélemy and Villefranche-de-Lonchapt. Monpazier (1285) is built on a low hill overlooking the source of the river Dropt.

Sometimes walls were built to increase the natural protection afforded by such sites and occasionally even a castle. Domme is walled, with three gates on the southern approach side, and has a now-ruined castle. Beaumont has walls which were added about fifty years after the town was founded, indicative of a worsening political situation in the early fourteenth century. Monpazier was once walled but they were later taken down and used to fill in the surrounding moat which, in the absence of strong natural defences, had given the town some protection. The effect has been to create an open space around the town used for games of *boule* or the occasional fair. In those towns which had no castle the church was enlarged, strengthened and fortified as a last line of defence. Windows were small and raised well above the ground. The huge church at Beaumont has an imposing tower, with arrow slits and machicolations, which dominates one corner of the square. Nearby Molières, though a much reduced town nowadays, has a similarly magnificent church.

Most bastides were built to a rectilinear plan and even in those which failed to attract population it is often possible to pick out the original design by tracing grass-grown paths intersecting at right angles. Sometimes these are almost the only clue on the ground to a settlement which either never succeeded or which became depopulated through war, disease or changed economic circumstances. Examples can be found at Beauregard, Monestier and Roquepine. Monpazier is the town which exhibits the most perfectly geometrical grid plan, rectangular in shape with three long and four short streets and a centrally located *place*. Villefranche-du-Périgord also has a

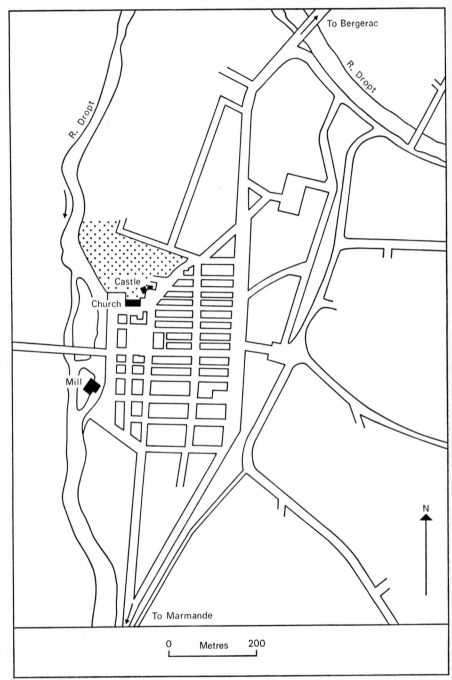

To Bergerac

R. Dropt

R. Dropt

Castle

Church

Mill

N

To Marmande

0    Metres    200

Fig 6    Eymet: a bastide town

regular layout with five north–south streets intersecting five others at right angles. Elsewhere, where local relief conditions imposed difficulties, the grid is likely to be less regular, with streets conforming to the contours—the chequers (or *ilôts*, ie spaces) between them varying in size. This is evident in the hilltop towns of Domme and Beaumont.

Long, narrow house plots were laid out within the chequers and these were often separated from each other by narrow passageways (*androne*s) giving access to premises at the rear which were added as the town prospered. Individual houses have been altered in the course of time, but it is not difficult to find buildings that are little changed from the thirteenth or fourteenth centuries. Within the town one whole *ilôt* was usually given over to the market place, another, or part of one, to the church. The *place* was the focal point of the town's life and still is in those bastides that have survived and retained their market functions. It would have a market hall, often of a fairly simple construction, with wooden piers supporting some kind of roof to give protection to the butter and other perishable foodstuffs, but because of the nature of the building few good examples have survived. Monpazier is an exception and the *halle* at Domme has also been restored.

Monpazier is also remarkable for the completeness of its *cornières* (galleried passages), perhaps the most distinctive of all the features of a typical bastide. The roads which enter the market place at its corners are continued beneath arcades formed by the projection of the upper storeys of shops and houses lining the square. Arches, some round, some pointed, give access to the *place* which has something of the appearance of a cloister, although the atmosphere, especially on market day or when some feast is celebrated, is far from being cloistered. Shops and cafés spill out beneath the arches and their tables mingle with market stalls to the despair of the motorist who forgets that the cornières were built for the wheeled traffic of the Middle Ages. In fact the carts of the fourteenth century prob-

E                                                                            69

ably had no less difficulty negotiating their entry to the *place*; at Monpazier the corners of the arcades have been cut away to permit direct access to the market place, but at Beaumont—where the cornières are less complete—it was necessary to turn at right angles beneath one of the arches and the confusion on market day is not difficult to imagine. Looking out from the cornières at Beaumont through one of the surviving city gates to the town fields beyond, it is not difficult to recapture something of the atmosphere of the Middle Ages.

### AN END TO ENGLISH RULE

The last bastide to be founded in Périgord was Saint-Barthélemy-de-Bellegarde in 1316. It can be said to mark the end of one of the most formative phases in the history of the region. That phase appears all the more remarkable in contrast with the long period of war, disease and impoverishment that was to follow.

Until the fourteenth century successive Dukes of Aquitaine had paid homage to the King of France as feudal overlord. It was a nominal loyalty and had not prevented wars breaking out over disputed territory, but the feudal game was generally played and it suited the English overlords in Aquitaine to set an example to the local barons who, in turn, owed allegiance to them. But in 1337 Edward III broke with medieval tradition, laying claim to the throne of France, and so gave rise to the Hundred Years War. Hostilities began in Aquitaine in 1345 and continued intermittently until 1453 with eventual defeat of the English on the banks of the Dordogne at Castillon and their expulsion from the south-west. Périgord was a frontier territory, and suffered internally from divided political loyalties, so that the long drawn out wars resulted in considerable hardship to the local population. Many settlements were destroyed and families were compelled to take refuge once more in the limestone caves and rock shelters.

Disease and famine added to the trials of the fourteenth century. The Black Death struck in 1348 but was only one of several outbreaks of the plague which killed large numbers. Over 1,300 people were taxed in Périgueux in 1366 but only about 800 by the end of the century. Uncertain harvests lowered resistance to disease and had long-term effects on the countryside. In particular, shortage of labour encouraged the spread of sharecropping (*métayage*), landowners hiring families whose term of employment fluctuated with the prevailing economic conditions. It was a time also when estates were bought up by merchants from the towns.

As before the barons were quick to turn the unsettled political state to their own advantage and we find, for example, the Count of Périgord challenging the authority of the French King in Périgueux. Towards the end of the fourteenth century the actions of Count Archambaud became so overbearing and oppressive towards the townspeople that the king was compelled to take action. Archambaud's town house in Périgueux and his castle at Montignac were besieged and in 1397 the count was banished from Périgord and his property confiscated. His son tried to regain the family estates by siding with the English but in turn was expelled from Montignac and the close of the fourteenth century marks the end of the comté of Périgord. Removal of the count served to weaken authority still further within the region and opened the way for outlaws and mercenaries to exploit the situation. Gangs under leaders like Ramonet de Sors terrorised the countryside where they came to be known as *brigands* after the name of their coat of mail—*la brigandine*. It was an inglorious end to the Middle Ages in Périgord.

# 4 RENAISSANCE AND REFORMATION

DEFEAT and expulsion of the English from Aquitaine was followed by a period of relative calm during which resettlement and rebuilding gradually took place. Towards the end of the fifteenth century the ideas of the Italian Renaissance began to enter France and provided the local gentry with a good excuse to add a new wing, a tower or, in some cases, to rebuild their house or castle in its entirety. This is nowhere better seen than in Périgord, a land of 'squires' whose traditional rivalry expressed itself now in castles, manors and town houses. Since the style of the Renaissance is described in Chapter 8, a single example will serve to illustrate the rebuilding movement. At Bourdeilles a thirteenth-century castle and sixteenth-century manor house stand side by side on a limestone cliff above the Dronne, both within the same perimeter wall. The old castle is dominated by its tall octagonal keep. The mansion is a rather austere building externally except for its porch with columns representing the three classical orders, but the interior is lavishly decorated with panelling, wall paintings and tapestries. It was built by Jacquette de Montbron in anticipation of a visit from the Queen Mother, Catherine de Médicis, who in fact never came, and the building was left unfinished.

The spirit of inquiry that gave rise to the renaissance in art and architecture is also to be seen in the Reformation of the sixteenth century. But the Reformation was also a reaction against the lax and worldly state of the Church at this time and in France it took the form of Calvinism. Its inspiration came

72

from the work of Jean Cauvin (Calvin) and the well-organised nature of the new Protestant order contrasted with the undisciplined character of the Catholic Church. Bourdeilles furnishes another example of the latter in the person of Pierre de Bourdeilles (1535–1614), brother-in-law to Jacquette de Montbron. As a younger son he had little prospect of advancement at home and so, at the age of sixteen, was made titular abbot at nearby Brantôme. Yet his life was the antithesis of that of the pious clergyman. He was an adventurer, a swashbuckling courtier who compares well with D'Artagnan, and he used the income deriving from his position at Brantôme to finance his travels round Europe in the service of the distinguished families of his day. They took him to Naples, Madrid and, in the company of Mary Queen of Scots, to Edinburgh. He met Queen Elizabeth in London and, back home in France, served under the rival families of Valois and Guise. Until he reached the age of fifty-four his life was 'one perpetual running to and fro in search of blood and battle' (Bentham-Edwards), but in that year a riding accident left him crippled and he returned to the abbey at Brantôme to write his memoirs and satisfy his lingering taste for adventure by engaging in lawsuits. His *Vie des Grands Capitaines* and *Dames Galantes*, written under the name of 'Brantôme', are full of risqué historical anecdotes and are presented in a lively style which suggests that age and infirmity had not reduced their author's zest for life. Brantôme's house has disappeared but the abbey church, a fine eleventh-century bell tower and other monastic buildings remain to provide a visible link with the past.

Protestantism gathered strength in France after the publication of Calvin's *Christianae Religionis Institutio* in 1536 and was strongest in the towns. In Périgord, Bergerac became the principal centre of *la réforme* and the tradition has remained strong there despite the exodus of Huguenots (the Protestants' popular name) which followed the repeal of the Edict of Nantes

73

in 1685. Modern Bergerac has a brisk, tidy, well-organised air about it which betrays its Calvinist background. At first the Protestant movement was wholly religious but as the sixteenth century progressed it became increasingly political and after 1559 was closely identified with the fortunes of the Bourbon family—Kings of Navarre—in their opposition to the family of Guise, rival claimants to the throne of France. The throne was held until 1589 by the Valois family, but the monarchy was constantly threatened during the last thirty years of this period. A succession of weak kings reigned, sons of Catherine de Médicis whose political skills were devoted to maintaining the unity of the kingdom in the face of many threats. The 'Wars of Religion' broke out in 1562 and lasted until 1598 when Henry of Navarre, who had succeeded to the throne as Henry IV in 1589, established freedom of worship under the Edict of Nantes.

The wars were particularly severe in the south-west where support for Henry of Navarre was strongest, and Périgord was subjected to the destruction and cruelty that had characterised the Hundred Years War. Armies lived off the land and ravaged the peasant holdings. Local loyalties were also divided. The lords of Bourdeilles supported the Catholic cause but Beynac was Protestant. At Biron the family was divided amongst itself; one of its sons, Charles de Gontaut, fought on the side of Henry of Navarre, achieving high office, but later betrayed him and was finally executed for treason in 1602. Similar divisions existed amongst the townspeople; Monpazier which is close to Biron was Protestant, but Beaumont to the north and Villefranche to the south were both Catholic towns. Recent violence in Northern Ireland gives one some idea of the situation that prevailed in Périgord during the second half of the sixteenth century.

Plague added to the suffering brought about by war and famine and a severe outbreak caused many deaths in Périgord in 1585. The hardship of the poor was observed by the essayist,

Montaigne, who saw something noble and virtuous in the struggles of the peasants to support their families:

> The poor folk whom one sees all around, head bowed after their day's work, who have no knowledge of Aristotle or Cato, of example or precept, from them nature daily draws examples of constancy and patience which are far more pure and enduring than those afforded to us by the scholars whom we study so avidly at school.

Michel Eyquem was a member of a merchant family which had bought the property at Montaigne in the lower Dordogne valley in 1477. 'Montaigne' himself was a man of business and was mayor of Bordeaux between 1581 and 1585, but his retreat was the family estate and it was here that he put together the ideas and observations that make up his three volumes of *Essays*. The castle tower which housed his library and study is still there and can be visited. From this he watched the peasants at their work and expressed his sympathy for their hard life. In Périgord, where he tends to be referred to as 'notre Montaigne', it is still common practice to include a quotation from his works in a formal speech, some indication of the respect which he gained by his identification with the poor and their problems at a time when most landowners had little interest in the land except for profit or sport.

Not all peasants, however, were content to suffer and be exploited, and towards the end of the century there was a wave of protest and rebellion. Those who rebelled were known as *croquants*, a word that translates freely as 'wretches', and the first outbreak of violence took place in 1594. Faced with this insurrection, the nobles—both Protestant and Catholic— joined together under the leadership of the Vicomte de Bourdeilles, the king's seneschal in Périgord, and the croquant revolt was soon crushed. But they were granted a number of tax concessions by Henry IV, a greater and more understanding king than any that had preceded him during the sixteenth century. Nevertheless by 1635 the croquants were again in revolt, this time against taxes imposed by Richelieu, chief minister to Henry's son, the ineffective Louis XIII. They were again defeated, in battles at Monpazier and Eymet, but a band of peasants under the leadership of Pierre Grelety held out in the Forêt de Vergt in central Périgord and carried on a successful guerrilla resistance for several years. Grelety was finally granted a royal pardon in 1643 and became a captain in the king's army.

Périgordins pride themselves on their dislike of authority and their respect for liberty. The croquants are respected for embodying this desire for freedom. The same feeling is represented in the work of Montaigne's contemporary and friend, Etienne de La Boétie who was born at Sarlat in 1530. His *Discours sur la Servitude Volontaire* is an appeal for human freedom that has been compared with Rousseau's *Contrat Social* and it may have helped to inspire the croquant revolt. A century later Périgord produced another publicist in the person of Fénelon, François de Salignac, who was born at the Château de Fénelon in the Dordogne valley above Domme in 1651. He expressed in his writing his opposition to absolute authority as represented by Louis XIV and, well ahead of his time, showed himself aware of the problems that can arise from over-centralised government. Like those of Montaigne, his views were based on a knowledge of local and regional affairs and, not without significance, the statues of the two men stand side by side in the Allées de Tourny in Périgueux at the present day.

### LES CYCLOPES QUI ENTRETIENNENT CES FEUX*

The second half of the seventeenth century brought fresh troubles to Périgord. In 1651 the region was fought over during the *Fronde*, a revolt of the nobility against the authority of Mazarin, chief minister to the youthful Louis XIV; later it

* Description of a Périgord ironworks by a visitor in 1730.

suffered from the persecution of the Protestants. The latter culminated in the revocation of the Edict of Nantes in 1685, denying to the Huguenots those freedoms of worship and involvement in public affairs that they had previously enjoyed. Many fled the region and the country, and the growth of Bergerac in particular was stunted by the loss of this skilled and enterprising section of its population. Yet despite these setbacks, gradual economic progress took place, and by the middle of the eighteenth century Périgord was enjoying a greater measure of prosperity than it had experienced for some 500 years. The bases of this prosperity were a more varied agriculture, exploitation of the region's forest wealth, and the iron industry.

During the seventeenth century the cultivation of maize— Spanish corn as it was known—was adopted in many parts of the region, the advantage of diversification being brought home in the last decade of the century when a series of bad harvests seriously affected the traditional cereal crops of rye and millet. The latter were used to bake a coarse brown bread (*pain bis*); maize was generally fed to animals, pigs and geese in particular, but if the need arose it could be used as a substitute for flour. If all else failed there were chestnuts which, like the maize, were usually eaten by pigs but were a useful source of flour in an emergency.

Walnut-growing had become established in Périgord by the seventeenth century. At that time walnuts were most important in the south, where Sarlat was the principal centre from which oil was sent to Bordeaux for export to England and Holland. Elsewhere they satisfied a domestic need for cooking oil and were a source also of oil for lighting. The potato was slow to be adopted and only became popular towards the end of the eighteenth century when roots and crops such as clover began to be included in rotations, reducing the need for a biennial fallow.

These examples suggest that peasant agriculture was being

77

gradually established on a securer basis than before. Out of a willingness to experiment with new crops evolved the pattern of *polyculture*—mixed crop and tree cultivation—which has remained typical to the present day. But it must not be supposed that the ordinary family was thereby much better off. The danger of starvation may have been reduced, but a typical day's diet in eighteenth-century Périgord still consisted of two meals of soup made from vegetables and a little salt pork, eaten with coarse bread that had been rubbed with onion or garlic. It was not very different in the nineteenth century when the regional novelist, Eugène Le Roy, described a peasant meal in *Jacquou le Croquant* (1899):

> My father cut three morsels of bread, reluctantly leaving the mouldiest piece and throwing it to the dog, then we made a pretence of dining. There wasn't much difference between our meal and that of the pig: it was always potatoes boiled in water; only in our dinner there was a bit of rancid dripping, as big as a walnut, and some salt.

Viticulture was stimulated after the middle of the seventeenth century by the growth of the Dutch market. They took principally white wines, whilst the English remained loyal to their red clarets. The effect was to extend vine cultivation throughout Aquitaine, and Périgord shared in the general expansion. Vines came to be grown far more widely than they are at the present day and the portion of the Dordogne valley around Domme, for example—unimportant now—contributed to the large trade of that valley in wines. Further north, the valleys of the Isle and the Dronne and those of their tributaries shared in the general prosperity. The rivers played a major role in the transport of wine as they did of other commodities such as walnut oil, chestnuts, timber, iron and salt. Towns, particularly those on the Dordogne, competed with each other for trade, their merchants sometimes refusing to handle the wines exported by a rival centre. Navigation on the river was improved to accommodate the growth in traffic and credit must be given to Colbert for having initiated work of this kind during his ascendancy as Louis XIV's minister in the third quarter of the seventeenth century.

During the course of the seventeenth and eighteenth centuries the form of land tenure that emerged as the most typical in Périgord was *métayage* (sharecropping), a form of leasehold under the terms of which the lessee paid his rent in produce, maybe a quarter, a third or even a half of the total crop, depending on the nature of the agreement. Landowners divided their properties for leasing into units of probably 20 to 30 hectares and looked forwards to enjoying fresh food without the trouble of cultivating the land themselves. Indeed some of them were townsmen living in Périgueux, Sarlat, Bergerac or one of the smaller towns. It was a system which offered a measure of security and that explains its popularity. To the landowner or the townsman with money to invest in land, it gave freedom from rapid falls in the value of money; to the *métayer* (or *colon* as he was sometimes called) it provided a means of entering farming without any capital and, where permanent contracts were entered into, security of tenure. For these reasons it was well suited to a relatively poor region such as Périgord. Its principal disadvantage was that, as short-term leases became more common, it did little to bring about improvement of the land, encouraging short-term profit rather than investment.

Despite the advances made in agriculture, large parts of Périgord were still forested in the eighteenth century, as indeed they still are. Except along the valleys and in the more fertile portions of Périgord Blanc and the Bergeracois, the agricultural landscape was one of forest clearings, quite unlike the extensive tracts of open *champagne* in northern France. But the forest, chiefly of oak and chestnut, also had a part to play in the regional economy. It was a source of food; it provided timber which was sent to Bordeaux for shipbuilding or the making of barrels; and within the region it supported paper and iron-making industries.

There are records which trace papermaking in Périgord back to the fifteenth century when the introduction of printing provided an early stimulus to the industry and by the eighteenth century it was well established in two localities. One of them was in the valley of the Isle near Thiviers where that river leaves the crystalline rocks and enters the limestone country of central Périgord. Here the attraction lay in the pure lime-free quality of the water and the presence of numerous power sites for driving watermills. The other locality was the Dordogne valley immediately above Bergerac together with that of the tributary river Couze which flows near to Beaumont-du-Périgord and joins the Dordogne below Lalinde. There was an outlier of this latter papermaking district further upstream in the valley of the Nouze which joins the Dordogne at Siorac. Here the water was less free of lime, though not heavily impregnated; there were power sites, even in the main valley, where they were fed by springs, and the Dordogne itself was an important routeway. Rags were the raw material used for papermaking until the nineteenth century when wood cellulose was substituted. It was then that the forest resources of the region began to be exploited, enabling these two old-established paper-making districts to survive the transition to modern industrial conditions. Access to new sources of raw material also led to the creation of a third centre of the industry at Condat near Terrasson in the upper valley of the Vézère.

The iron industry was even more closely identified with local materials than was papermaking, being entirely dependent on local ores and on a supply of charcoal from the forests. It has a long history in the region, small deposits of ironstone having been worked intermittently from pre-Roman times to supply the simple bloomeries which made iron for tools or arms. But it expanded considerably in the eighteenth century, especially after 1750 when the demand for armaments was greatly increased as a result of French involvement in the Seven Years War. It survived until as late as 1930 when the last charcoal-fired blast furnace was blown out at Savignac-Lédrier in the upper valley of the Auvézère near Lanouaille. To the industrial archaeologist, this and other sites in the Nontronnais of northern Périgord afford ample opportunities for exploring the remains of forges, furnaces and the 'hammer-ponds' that provided power for the waterwheels.

Iron-making was not confined to the uplands of north-eastern Périgord. In the Vézère valley and elsewhere there were small ironworks based on local deposits of ore and the charcoal that could be obtained from nearby woods. But the greater part of the industry was to be found in valleys like that of the Bandiat and the headwaters of the Dronne, Isle and Auvézère which drain the crystalline plateaux of the north. Here were ideal power sites, together with fairly easy access to supplies of both ore and charcoal. There are many small lakes which afford natural reservoirs and, in addition, the deeply incised valleys could be dammed at various points to provide a head of water for the furnace bellows and for driving the power hammers. Furnaces and forges therefore were strung out along the valleys making full use of the available water supply and of the best power sites.

Small amounts of ore were to be found close to these valley sites in the form of kidney ores which occur randomly in the thin deposits of Tertiary sands and clays covering some of the plateau tops. Most of the iron, though, came from ironstone bands within the outcrop of Jurassic rocks which fringes the uplands to the south. Here, around Javerlhac, Nontron and Excideuil, the ores were worked in open pits and then transported by mule or oxcart to the furnace sites. Largely non-phosphoric, the ores had an iron content of some 35 to 40 per cent and about 3 tons were required for each ton of iron produced.

A few furnaces were set up close to the ore quarries, mainly in

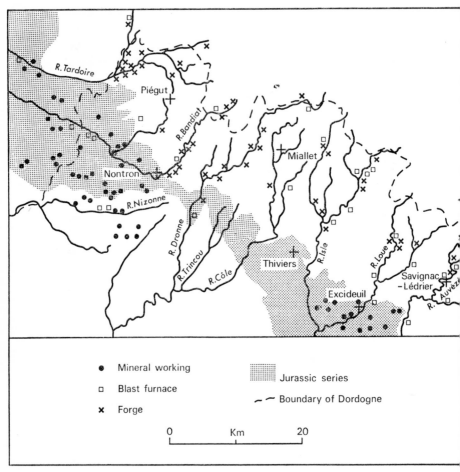

Fig 7    Iron industry of the Nontronnais (after René Pijassou, *Rev Géog des Pyrénées et du S-O,* 1956)

the valley of the Bandiat where it turns north-westwards and flows along the outcrop of the Jurassic rocks. These were ideally sited from the point of view of access to ore and account for the importance of Javerlhac as a centre of the industry. Elsewhere the cost of transporting ore added significantly to the iron-maker's total costs, the price frequently doubling over the distance of 10 or even fewer kilometres between quarry and furnace. The burden was increased by the cost of obtaining charcoal, of moving the iron from furnace to forge and of transporting the finished products. Charcoal was obtained from nearby forests, the ironmasters owning tracts of forest land within which they employed charcoal-burners to prepare the fuel for them, but when the industry was prosperous and consuming large quantities of material it was inevitable that the charcoal would have to be carried over greater distances. Limestone for fluxing also had to be carried to the furnace sites that were away from the outcrop of Jurassic rocks.

Many different kinds of ironware were manufactured in Périgord during the heyday of the industry in the late-eighteenth and early-nineteenth centuries. They included domestic utensils and hardware, agricultural equipment and edge tools. Frying-pans were a speciality of the upper Bandiat valley and Nontron, a town which benefited greatly from the growth of the iron industry, still makes knives. A number of slitting mills were also set up to manufacture rods for purposes such as nail-making. Most of these goods supplied what was essentially a regional market in Périgord and adjacent parts of the south-west, but for one group of products the industry acquired a national reputation; this was for naval artillery—cannon, mortars, gun carriages, shot etc. Rochefort was the big naval base to which the artillery had to be transported. This involved an overland journey—fortunately downhill most of the way—to Ruelle and then to l'Humeau, a suburb of Angoulême on the Charente, where it was loaded on boats for transport to the sea. Ruelle, a few kilometres from Angoulême, had been established as an iron-making centre in 1750 and subsequently became the *Fonderie Nationale de la Marine*, the place from which the supply of artillery from this part of Angoumois and from Périgord was organised.

The manufacture of artillery made the fortunes of a number of *maîtres de forges* in the second half of the eighteenth century. In Périgord the leading personalities in the industry were Louis Blanchard de Sainte-Catherine and François de Laponge, both of whom owned several forges as well as extensive lands that were leased to métayers. But in addition to these captains of industry there were many small forge owners who were responsible for the range of smaller goods noted above. On the whole it was these small-scale iron-makers who ensured the survival of the industry into the twentieth century, for the demand for cannon was a fluctuating one and the manufacturers who specialised in this kind of equipment soon lost their fortunes. Transport costs were always a burden to them and, as demand slackened or payments for some reason or another were withheld, the ironmasters were thrown increasingly into debt. In general the industry was under-capitalised, which brought about its eventual collapse. When railways were built, Périgord iron could no longer compete in price with that made under modern methods using coke in other parts of France. But a site like Savignac-Lédrier, some distance from the railways, was able to survive until 1930 by specialising in simple products for an exclusively local market.

## REVOLUTION

The Revolution of 1789 did not bring about a completely new social order in Périgord. The lands of churchmen and nobles were confiscated and offered for sale but this was to the benefit of the bourgeoisie who could afford to buy them rather than to the peasants. For the latter, the Revolution was an opportunity to settle some old scores and a number of castles were sacked,

*Page 85*
Bastide of Beaumont-du-Périgord: two views of the thirteenth-century Porte du Luzier

Page 86   (above) *Cornières* and market place at Monpazier; (below) Bourdeilles: the thirteenth-century keep and unfinished Renaissance manor

including Biron. But in general the peasants achieved little more than freedom from the more irksome and antiquated feudal ties and many of them continued to work as métayers or farm labourers. As the nineteenth century progressed there was a shift of ownership in favour of the peasant proprietor, but the move was a relatively slow one until after the agricultural crisis of the 1870s.

An immediate product of the Revolution, however, was a new system of local government, which is of interest in illustrating how completely the territorial unity of Périgord had survived the wars and rebellions of preceding centuries. One of the objects of the National (or Constituent) Assembly elected in 1789 was to substitute a national system of administration for the confused pattern of provincial authorities inherited from the *ancien régime*. Accordingly France was divided into eighty-three départements of which one, Dordogne, corresponded broadly in outline with historic Périgord, the officers of the Assembly who were responsible for the new boundaries showing themselves to be remarkably sensitive to the strength of local feeling.

The extent of the new département is best compared with that of the ancient diocese since this, rather than the comté, had survived the rigours of time. True, in 1317, one of the Avignon popes, John XXII, had created a separate diocese of Sarlat, but the latter had remained closely associated with that of Périgueux and in 1790 the two were reunited without any territorial changes. The boundaries of diocese and département are represented on Fig 1, which shows that portions of territory were lost to the départements of Charente and Lot-et-Garonne in the north-west and south-west respectively, but these losses were balanced by the addition of Nontronnais in the north and a portion of the Causse in the south-east. On the whole the adjustments can be explained in terms of political loyalties that had developed during the centuries of feudal authority. The strength of such ties is well illustrated by the transfer in 1792 of eleven communes from the département of Corrèze to that of Dordogne. Though not within the diocese of Périgueux, these communes in the upper Auvézère valley had strong economic and social links with neighbouring parts of Périgord—they included, for example, Savignac-Lédrier—and a plea that their ties should be recognised by inclusion in Dordogne was upheld.

It is clear that in spite of its turbulent history the Dordogne region of France has exhibited an extraordinary ability to survive as a definable entity. In seeking to explain this the role of the church must be stressed, but account must also be taken of the strength of tradition and the social and economic links which the network of rivers has helped to create and maintain. Such associations, between ordinary people at the local level, have proved stronger in the long run than the effects of political division and war. In the words of the historian, Camille Julian, 'Périgord affords one of the best examples of continuity that can be found in the historical geography of Gaul.'

Having defined the new départements, the task of the Constituent Assembly was to select a *chef-lieu* to house the *préfecture*, the administrative headquarters. Périgueux's claim to serve as capital of Dordogne was challenged by both Bergerac and Sarlat, which, at that time, were of almost equal size. Wishing to be fair to all, the Assembly therefore hit on the idea of a rotating capital, each of the three towns to serve as chef-lieu in turn. It was an impractical solution. Périgueux was chosen to act first and, in fact, has retained the role ever since. The advantages of Périgueux's central position and easier access to the whole of the département ensured that the town would continue to exercise the administrative function that it has had throughout history. Some compensation was found for Bergerac and Sarlat in being made minor administrative centres, *sous-préfectures*, together with Nontron and Ribérac. The boundaries of the *arrondissements* which they controlled corresponded broadly with those of the major river basins and the division of the département in this way mirrored closely the older divisions of Périgord into tribal territories and baronies. Historical continuity is again evident, even at the sub-regional level.

During the first half of the nineteenth century the population of the département of Dordogne increased by almost 25 per cent, from a total of 409,445 in 1801, to 505,789 in 1851. The iron industry was still active in the north-east and agriculture still benefited from a willingness to experiment with new crops and techniques.

A lead was given by certain pioneering landlords, prominent amongst whom were the Marquis de Fayolle on his estate at Tocane-Saint-Apre in the valley of the Dronne, and the Maréchal Bugeaud, a retired army officer from the Napoleonic wars who bought the estate of La Durantie near Lanouaille in 1819. In his campaigns, Bugeaud had observed the improvements that were being made to farms in northern France and elsewhere and he introduced most of them at La Durantie. When he took over in 1819 the biennial fallow was still commonly practised and there was evidence of a still more primitive system, a form of shifting cultivation in fact, under which the land was farmed for three or four successive years and then left to recover under scrub and forest for a period of at least twenty years. Bugeaud did away with the necessity for a fallow, introducing clover and root crops in rotation and increasing the number of stock, which in turn produced manure to enrich the fields. He also planted vines and improved the quality of his forest land by planting oaks and chestnuts. Other farmers were impressed by the much higher yields that he was able to get from his crops and there was a gradual diffusion of the new methods through the rural community. The changes, however, were largely absorbed within an organisation that remained wedded to métayage and polyculture and it would be wrong to suppose that all landlords were as progressive as Bugeaud.

The amount of land devoted to vines continued to increase during the nineteenth century and reached a maximum in Périgord of 110,000 hectares in 1872. They were grown by landowners, métayers and farm labourers alike, and the attention required for the cultivation of the vine ensured a corresponding increase in population in those areas devoted to the crop. They were common on the slopes of the lower Dordogne valley around Bergerac, but of much greater interest is their importance in those parts of Périgord where comparatively few vines are grown now: the Ribéracois, the Causse, the Sarladais and the country south of the Dordogne around Domme.

In some localities the vine occupied more land than all the field crops together and the slopes of many limestone hills were literally covered with vines. Verteillac was the centre of vine-growing in the 'downland' country of Périgord Blanc. Savignac-les-Eglises was at the heart of a major wine-producing district on the Causse which extended from Villars and Saint-Jean-de-Côle in the north through Sorges and Agonac as far as La Bachellerie and Terrasson in the south. Good wines were produced here, most of which made their way to the Limousin, passing through the market towns such as Excideuil and Hautefort which border the upland country. The agricultural landscape of the Limousin was being transformed by an increasing emphasis on pastoralism and the mid-nineteenth century was a time of great activity for these little towns which acted as exchange centres between the contrasting pays to north and south.

Another notable wine-producing district was that extending southwards from Sarlat through Domme to Daglan, Campagnac and Saint-Pompon. The geological maps show that these latter villages are situated on a narrow strip of limestone causse, widening out towards the border of Quercy and drained by the river Céou. The slopes of this river basin were clothed with vines and the wine made from them was sent both up and down the Dordogne from small ports on the river like Castelnaud or Cénac.

Except perhaps in the major river valleys, agricultural land in the Dordogne tends to give the impression of having been won from the forest, and the extent of the forest cover at a particular time is a good barometer to the state of agricultural prosperity. As a result of progress made in vine growing and other forms of agriculture, the forest occupied soon after the middle of the nineteenth century an area of land that was probably smaller than at any previous time. There was also less forest then than now. René Pijassou has calculated the forest area at 22 per cent of the whole, with another 7 or 8 per cent devoted to the chestnut, the land given over to which was calculated separately because of the special role of the chestnut as a source of food. Individual tracts of forest were still sufficiently well defined to have local names, however: the Forêt de Vergt, the Forêt Barade etc.

Agricultural prosperity lasted until the 1870s, then came collapse, ruin and emigration. In 1881 the population of Dordogne still totalled 495,037; by the turn of the century it had fallen to 452,951 (1901) and in 1921 the total was only 396,742. A fifth of the population had been lost in forty years. In the countryside the loss was greater than this since the overall figures obscure the movement that was taking place to the towns in search of work. The towns could not support large numbers, however, and many left the region altogether, going to Bordeaux and Paris or abroad, many of them to Latin America.

Several reasons account for the depression that precipitated the loss of population. Locally grown wheat was less able to compete after 1870 with imported American wheats which depressed prices. There were bad harvests. The advent of the railway had far-reaching effects, not only on the iron industry, but on the regional economy as a whole. It ended, for example, the lucrative waterborne traffic on the Dordogne, the line up the valley reaching Bergerac in 1875 and Le Buisson, where it meets the main line from the north, in 1879. But the greatest disaster was phylloxera, the insect pest that destroyed the vineyards.

Phylloxera was introduced to France on infected stock from America in the early 1860s. Vines lost their leaves and died but it was some years before the cause became known, the reason being that the phylloxera aphid feeds on the roots of the vine. By the time the dead vine was dug up and inspected the insects had moved on to other plants which, above ground, seemed as yet to be unaffected and which the farmers were therefore loathe to uproot. By the time the nature of the phylloxera was fully understood the pest had spread so widely that little could be done to check it. In Périgord the worst ravages occurred in the late 1870s and by 1892 the area of land devoted to vines had fallen to under 22,000 hectares, only a fifth of that recorded twenty years earlier.

In time a number of ways were discovered of combating the phylloxera: flooding the vineyards, injecting carbon bisulphide into the earth around the roots, and grafting on to resistant American rootstock. They were expensive solutions, and limestone hillsides could not be flooded. In Périgord only the Bergeracois managed to recover from phylloxera. A few examples can be found in other parts of Périgord of estates that were bought, usually by outsiders, and vines replanted, but such schemes were exceptional and commercial viticulture has generally been given up even on these estates during the present century. Elsewhere, with the exception of a few rows here and there for purely domestic needs, the vineyards were never replanted, and the effect on large areas of the Causse, the Sarladais and, to a lesser degree, the Ribéracois, was catastrophic. Farms were abandoned and scrub forest once again invaded the clearings of cultivated land. Métayers had insufficient capital to embark on any alternative form of commercial agriculture and those who remained took refuge in subsistence polyculture. What little money they had was devoted to acquiring a small holding of their own as the bigger properties were divided up and sold.

The severity of the crisis in the final decades of the nineteenth century would have been less if there had been any corresponding growth in industrial employment, but such was not the case. Closure of most of the remaining charcoal ironworks added to the population loss and there was no coal available to serve as a basis for industrialisation. Craft industries suffered competition from the more cheaply produced goods that could now be brought in by railway. Some enterprising proprietors began to plant pines on the old vineyards or on scrubland and their example was followed by others. The trees were tapped for resin and they also supported small sawmills, but the amount of employment created was only small.

Migration is usually age-selective, and it tended to be the younger and more vigorous sections of the community who left Périgord in the years before World War I, leaving the older and less enterprising to manage the land. The effect of the Great War was similar, robbing the region of its young people. The effect was to depress the birth rate, from around 20 per thousand in the third quarter of the nineteenth century to 15 per thousand in the early years of the present one, and no more than 13 to 14 per thousand between the wars. By this time there were annually more deaths than births. In the Sarladais the density of population, which was 374 per thousand hectares in 1886, had fallen to only 106 per thousand hectares by 1926.

An increasingly elderly population in the countryside made it difficult to effect any kinds of agricultural reforms and a scheme was embarked upon in the 1920s to bring groups of Breton farmers to Périgord. It was hoped by so doing to solve two problems, overpopulation in Brittany and underpopulation in Périgord. Some 10,000 Bretons were brought under this arrangement. There was also a trickle of migrants from the north under the threat of war, the overall effect of which was to check the absolute decline of numbers in the region. The census of 1946 recorded a population of 387,643, nine thousand fewer than in 1921.

Loss of population has continued since World War II despite an increase in the birth rate here as in other parts of France. The total had fallen to 377,870 in 1954, to 375,455 in 1962 and, at the last census in 1968, to 374,073. During this latest inter-censal period the planning region of Aquitaine, of which Dordogne is a part, experienced an increase in population of 6·3 per cent. The continued loss of population from the Dordogne is all the more remarkable for the fact that the département absorbed over 9,000 repatriates from North Africa during the 1960s. It is evident that the drift from the countryside is still taking place in Périgord and it is not surprising that so many properties have come on the market as 'second homes' during the last few years. Yet despite this rather depressing story there is evidence of progress in some aspects of the regional economy, so long in decline. They will be highlighted in the following chapters which look at the nature of this economy.

# 5                    UN PEU DE TOUT

MORE than a quarter of a century has elapsed since Philip Oyler wrote *The Generous Earth*, that charming and nostalgic account of life amongst the peasant families of the Dordogne valley. Many changes have taken place during this time and rural depopulation has robbed the country-side, not only of sons and daughters, but of whole families. There has been a positive side to change too. Farms have been mechanised and there is a greater degree of specialisation in what is produced. The outlook is more commercial and new crops have been introduced such as strawberries which are marketed through co-operative societies. A cash income has made it possible to carry out improvements to the home—they usually begin in the kitchen—and with piped water gradually being added to the now almost universal supply of electricity, domestic life is more comfortable; some would say a little less picturesque.

Not all is changed, however, and one does not have to travel far in Périgord to see examples of that most traditional of peasant responses to his environment, polyculture, 'un peu de tout', a little of everything—or 'beaucoup de rien' as its critics have tended to say of it. As Oyler observed, 'the agricultural technique of the people (of the Dordogne valley) cannot be considered apart from the main characteristics of their civilisa-tion as a whole, nor from their mentality, nor even from their spirituality, indefinable though this may be. Integration is in fact the outstanding characteristic of that civilisation: the agri-cultural technique is fitted into the whole structure.' Or to put

95

it more simply, 'If you have a bit of everything, you are not dependent on anyone.' It is a philosophy that appeals to the peasant farmer who cherishes his independence.

### POLYCULTURE

Suppose there were such a thing as an average farm. It has 10 hectares of land but four of these are under a rather scrubby woodland and the cultivated plots are of varying size and shape and are distributed in several different fields. The woodland is useful as a source of fuel for the kitchen stove; mushrooms can be collected there provided one gets up early enough in the morning, and there is a stand of pines that will be sold when some extra cash is needed to replace the tractor. Half the cultivated land is under cereals, mainly wheat for domestic use, but the baker who calls three times a week has lessened the need for home-baked bread and the tendency is therefore to grow more barley and maize for animal feed. Wheat, though, may still be exchanged with the baker under an agreement by which he supplies bread free of charge. Maize has become popular since World War II following the introduction of better-yielding, hybrid strains and a couple of old farm carts with high sides have been made into maize silos with wire netting and these stand in the farmyard ready for use during the winter.

Wheat is harvested in July if the weather permits and is followed by a crop of clover or lucerne that was undersown with it, or else some other kind of *culture dérobée* is planted, roots or quick-growing buckwheat. One plot is given over to vines, again to satisfy the needs of the family who also make good use of the climbers (*en baradis*) which look so attractive in front of the house. One of these is an early, dessert variety; the other ripens later and makes a good liqueur. Haricots verts and carrots are grown between a number of rows of vines (*en hautins*) and there are more amongst the maize, together with a pumpkin or two. The remainder of the land is given over to a variety of crops: potatoes, beets, peas, broad beans and cabbage; many of them go to make soup. There is a patch of *salade* and artichokes and, where the soil is sandy, a few rows of asparagus and perhaps a little tobacco. A number of gnarled fruit trees grow on the hill slope—probably apples, plums and cherries—and scattered here and there in the fields are walnuts, like the tobacco a small but useful source of cash income. Crops are grown under the trees but the walnut casts a deep shade so that they do not yield particularly well there unless, like cabbage, they need protection from the sun.

Polyculture is mixed arable farming but that is not to say that livestock are absent. Oxen have given way to the tractor but a couple of cows may still be yoked together and taken out to the fields even if it is only to draw back a cart full of beets. Compared with a tractor they proceed 'plus doucement'. Our average farm keeps four or five cows which supply milk for the family and perhaps a little for sale; some cheese is also sold and occasionally there is a calf to market. The cattle are stall-fed in the winter but during the summer months they are taken each day to the meadow where the farmer has some grazing rights in common with his neighbours. A few pigs are fattened but these are rarely seen outside. By contrast the farmyard is never without some chickens, ducks and a few noisy guineafowl. There is a pen of geese but they, too, enjoy a good measure of freedom to forage for themselves until the time comes in November to fatten them up (*le gavage*) for *foie gras*. The picture is completed with a *pigeonnier* and a hutch or two of rabbits.

There is, of course, always an element of unreality about the 'average farm', and increasingly those farms that survive do so by specialisation. Yet the descriptive 'model' presented above still has a considerable degree of validity in Périgord as anyone who explores the countryside away from the main roads will soon discover. To Philip Oyler this system of farming, concerned above all with the immediate needs of the family, represented the good life:

> The general economy of the farm consists in producing a continuous succession of crops, providing an immense variety of food for man and beast. If variety is the spice of life, here it is in fullness. Such variety does not mean merely a wonderfully balanced diet. It means also a constant change of work, which makes that, too, far more interesting . . . And we pity the poor peasant. What a farce. While we talk about a higher standard of living, he has had for centuries a luxurious one.

Not everyone has interpreted polyculture in such favourable terms. Perhaps Oyler had not read Eugène Le Roy's *Jacquou le Croquant* or *L'Année Rustique*.

It would be wrong to account for polyculture only in human terms. Although human considerations have played a major part in the entrenchment of this system of agriculture, it must be seen also as a product of the great variety of physical conditions encountered within the region, particularly of soils, but also of microclimates which reflect the soil differences as well as those of slope and aspect.

At the regional level it is possible to make a broad distinction between soil types typical of the major physical divisions recognised in Chapter 2. The chalky marls of Périgord Blanc have very different qualities from the coarse, podsolic soils developed on the *sidérolithique* of central Périgord; the hungry sands of the Landais and the Double contrast with the molasses of the Bergeracois; the granular, acid soils of the Nontronnais give way to fine, sandy clays on the schists of Lanouaille and to fertile marls in the Lias basins; the thin stony soils of the Causse have little in common with the alluvium of the major river valleys. Some of these differences are encountered over remarkably short distances and the farmer with his scattered plots has been quick to take advantage of the contrasted opportunities afforded to him, but at this local level it is even more important to stress the contribution of relief. Périgord is not an upland region comparable with the Massif Central, but few parts of it are flat and the peasant farmer has long recognised a distinction between soils that are typical of the upper slopes— the *terreforts* or *pays forts*—and the *boulbènes* of the lower slopes.

Terreforts are clay soils with a high lime content, typically brown or yellow in colour. Towards the top of the slope the *terrefort maigre* is encountered, thin and pale coloured, but this grades lower down into darker *terreforts batârds* (mixed) and *terreforts lourds* which have the highest clay content. The mixture of clay and lime means that the terreforts drain reasonably well in wet weather and yet retain soil moisture in dry spells. They also resist erosion. For these reasons they are favoured as arable soils, despite a reputation amongst some farmers as soils 'difficile à prendre', ie they must be ploughed when the moisture balance in the soil is just right in order to avoid the clay particles cementing. If 'taken' then, however, they are not hard to work and after being broken up by winter frosts they yield well, especially when they have had a good application of manure to maintain their humus content. Soils very similar in type to these terreforts are the combe deposits which fill the bottoms of many small valleys including those that are now dry. They owe their origin to postglacial downwash, or solifluction, and have a clay matrix with fragments of limestone and possibly some lighter, sandy windblown material. Known as *castine* or *terreforts francs*, these easily-worked soils have been closely identified with the oases of cultivation won, over the years, from the forests of central Périgord.

Boulbènes are light, sandy soils (*terres douces*). They are generally associated with the river terraces but similar ones are developed on the sands and gravels which cap the forested hills of central Périgord and the Sarladais—Périgord Noir. They are loose in texture, easy to work but with a poor structure; according to the farmers they 'manquent de corps', lack body. When they are underlain by a hardpan layer they can become waterlogged in winter, but they also dry out easily in summer so that a careful balance between drainage and irrigation has to be maintained where they are utilised for orchards, as they are to an increasing extent in the Dordogne valley. Their humus content is low so that manure and fertilisers are essential to maintaining their fertility when they are cropped. A farmer will try to dung all his fields but these are the ones he must be sure to attend to, and he will be careful to include leguminous crops in his rotations. On the hills, the coarse gravelly soils have tended to be cultivated only when there has been a strong demand for land—under conditions of population pressure in the twelfth or thirteenth centuries or when vine-growing was profitable in the nineteenth century. At other times they have been left *en friche* (fallow) and recolonisation by the forest has gradually taken place. The introduction of strawberry cultivation since World War II has found a new use for these soils in central Périgord and favoured parts of the forest are once more giving way to the plough.

The climate of Périgord is favourable to a wide range of crops. There is a long growing season with high temperatures from June to early September (Périgueux: January mean 5° C, July mean 21° C), and although summer is the driest season there is none of the drought, dust and glare associated with a Mediterranean summer. Indeed the success of most of the crops depends on rain falling during summer. In terms of climatic means, the region may be described as one of increment. Averages, however, are misleading since they obscure the essentially fickle nature of Périgord's climate. Long, dry spells are by no means uncommon in summer and the growth of crops is then retarded unless irrigation water is available. When a dry period ends it is likely to do so with a sequence of dramatic storms, when soil is washed away and hail damages the fruit and tobacco crops.

Winter may be cold and dry but is more likely to be humid and relatively mild. Périgueux averages only three days of snowfall a year. Yet a mild winter is often succeeded by cold spring nights when frosts occur in the combes and valley bottoms. Foggy conditions are also relatively common, especially in the mornings. Farmers are aware of the advantages of slope and aspect, as they are of the contrasted qualities of the soils, but seasonal variations in weather conditions cannot be foreseen and a summer that is good for certain crops is far from ideal for others. Under such conditions the advantages of polyculture again manifest themselves to the peasant smallholder, and he has many proverbs that derive from his observations of the weather and climate. 'If it rains on Saint-Roch, there'll be a truffle on the rock.'

Subsistence polyculture was not new to the Dordogne region in the 1870s, but the economic and political crises of those years did much to consolidate its hold on the region's agriculture. Phylloxera, loss of markets for wheat, the weakness of the currency, bad harvests and years of starvation, compelled the peasant farmer to look to his own needs first. Land was worth more than cash and it was safer to grow one's own food than to seek to supply a distant and uncertain market in which profits usually went to the middleman rather than the grower. The peasant holding producing 'un peu de tout' became a centre of resistance in time of crisis. But there was another reason for polyculture that must be mentioned to complete the explanation and that was the fragmented nature of most farm holdings, a consequence, in part, of Napoleon's Civil Code which had required equal division of property between heirs. It was the scattered nature of his holding that permitted the peasant to exploit to the full the varied nature of his physical environment.

### REMEMBREMENT

There are nearly 40,000 farm holdings in Périgord including ones that are cultivated on a part-time basis. Eighty per cent of them are owner-occupied (*propriétaires*). Métayage, which re-

mained important up to World War II, has now largely disappeared and accounts for under 5 per cent of the holdings. On
some medium-sized properties it has given way to farm
tenancy (*fermiers*) but, in general, the former métayers have
been encouraged to acquire their own farm although this has
often meant obtaining some kind of credit loan. The average
size of holding is only 11 hectares, compared with the national
average of $14\frac{1}{2}$ hectares, but there are enormous variations in
farm size from the domaine with several hundred hectares run
on the most modern lines, to the tiny unit with under a hectare
of cultivable land. Thirty per cent of the farms, in fact, have
under 5 hectares. Such a situation is not new, a few large and
many small holdings having long been typical. Large properties
are more common on the hilly interfluves than in the rich river
valleys, but there is no very obvious pattern in their distribution,
and even in the former areas it is common to find clusters of
little farms adjacent to the big domaine which often affords part-
time work to the otherwise underemployed families.

Only rarely is one of these farm holdings, whether large or
small, made up of a compact block of fields. Most are highly
fragmented, with plots of different shapes and sizes existing
either as patches of cleared land within the forest or as strips
amongst the big, open fields. It has been estimated that there
were something like 3 million individual plots of land in the
Dordogne region in the mid-1950s. Such an enormous total
must certainly include the patches of land on which farm
buildings stand and which are demarcated separately on the
cadastral maps, yet if the total number of cultivated plots were
only half this figure it would still represent a high degree of
fragmentation.

Such *parcellement* has no single explanation. It is partly a
consequence of the inheritance laws, but it also reflects the
varied nature of the physical environment and it is closely
related to the tradition of polyculture described above. It does
not make for an efficient agriculture in the sense that time is lost

Page 103  (*above*) Strawberry cultivation on cleared forest land in central Périgord; (*below*) tobacco in the Dordogne valley

*Page 104*  (*above*) Deer released for restocking by the Fédération des Chasseurs;
(*below*) papermill at Port-de-Couze

walking between the scattered parcels of land, and their small size does not encourage the best use of machinery. Yet, in making judgements, it must be remembered that except at certain times of the year the peasant farmer often had time to spare, and labour-intensive crops such as vines and tobacco profited in terms of yield from the close attention that he was able to give to them.

On the wooded interfluves the plots of land are highly irregular in shape, corresponding usually with a patch of better soils. Dry stone walls are used to check the downward movement of soil on slopes; elsewhere the individual plots are usually separated by hedges studded with trees so that from a distance the appearance is still one of a well-wooded countryside. The river valleys, in contrast, display an open and more obviously man-made landscape. Hedges are rare, and the regularly shaped parcels combine with their crops to form an impressive mosaic of cultivated land. Rectangular forms predominate, with plots aligned parallel with, or at right angles to, the access roads. Their width is usually no more than a quarter of their length, and maybe only a tenth or even less on the gently sloping land within the broad valley meanders, the *cingles*, like that of the Dordogne at Trémolat. Here the long, narrow strips fan out like spokes of a wheel towards the river, facilitating drainage and reducing to a minimum the amount of cultivable land lost (the *talvère*) because of the need to turn the plough-team, or now, the tractor.

Elsewhere strips orientated north–south are more common than ones running east–west, since the former are warmed by both the morning and the evening sun and cold, shadowy spots are eliminated. Where plots are unfenced and all the land is cultivated, it is necessary for individual farmers to respect the rights of others and complicated clauses relating to access are written into contracts concerned with the sale of land. Because of these rights it is common to find the same crop grown on separate plots which happen to be served by the same right of access; elsewhere the pattern of land-use seems to defy analysis.

The inconveniences involved in farming many scattered parcels has encouraged some farmers to exchange land in order to create more compact holdings. Voluntary *remembrement* of this kind has been made easier by the drift of population from the land, though it would be quite wrong to suppose that the farmer who moves to the town will always sell or even rent out his land. Ask the old peasant farmer hoeing his potatoes where he lives and the reply may well be the nearest town, with his son or even in a home for old people. He has come out on the bus to spend the day on his 'lopin de terre'. The old farmhouse has been sold but he has kept the barn to store his tools and for making a little wine.

In 1941 the French Government set up a Service de Remembrement to promote the reorganisation of farms throughout the country. Funds and advice are made available at the level of the commune and the service has had considerable success in the areas of openfield agriculture (*grosse culture*) in northern France. In Périgord, however, the progress of planned remembrement has been much slower, due in part to more complicated physical and agricultural conditions, partly also to peasant suspicion of the ways of officials. A departmental commission for remembrement was not set up in Périgord until 1960 and it was the following year before the first Commission Communale was established—for the commune of Gouts-Rossignol in the Ribéracois. Here farm reorganisation was completed towards the end of 1963, a total of 1,615 plots (average size 1·3 hectares) having been reduced to 530 (average 4 hectares). Since that time remembrement has been carried out in other communes although most of them are confined to the western fringe of the département, to the wider, flatter river valleys, and the less wooded hills of the Ribéracois.

In other parts of the region remembrement has proved much more difficult to initiate. Where soil conditions are uniform it is not hard to persuade farmers to exchange plots, but when they vary over short distances, as is the case over much of the Dordogne region, suspicions are easily aroused, the more particularly since reallocation takes place on the basis of creating new holdings of equal productivity, not necessarily of equal size, to the old ones. The importance of tree crops, especially walnuts, also operates against remembrement. Scattered amongst the fields, underplanted with other crops and at varying stages of maturity, they make plot reallocation almost impossible to achieve. Where remembrement has taken place in the central or eastern parts of Périgord it has usually been in connection with some associated scheme for drainage, irrigation or the grubbing of forest land to extend the cultivated acreage. Such has been the case, for example, in the commune of Tamnies in the Sarladais. Some experts argue that in these areas of traditionally small-scale and mixed agriculture, remembrement is hardly worth attempting and funds are much better spent on the provision of a piped water supply.

If it is difficult to generalise about the value of remembrement, it is equally true of the value of farm mechanisation. Fewer than 2 per cent of the farmers in Périgord had a tractor at the end of World War II. Twenty years later the proportion was 50 per cent, and tractors are now used on almost all holdings except the very small ones. Other forms of farm machinery have also been adopted, but not everywhere successfully. Many instances can be found of under-used machines and of farmers who have run up debts in an excess of zeal for mechanisation. Some have turned to remembrement in an effort to make better use of their machinery; a few have pooled their resources, but the co-operative idea is slow to take root in this region of peasant smallholders. Change is taking place, spurred on by the advice of local organisations like the CIVAM (Centres d'Information et de Vulgarisation Agricole et Ménagère), but it is not always painless.

Polyculture survives, yet the last twenty years have been marked by increasing specialisation leading, in turn, to more

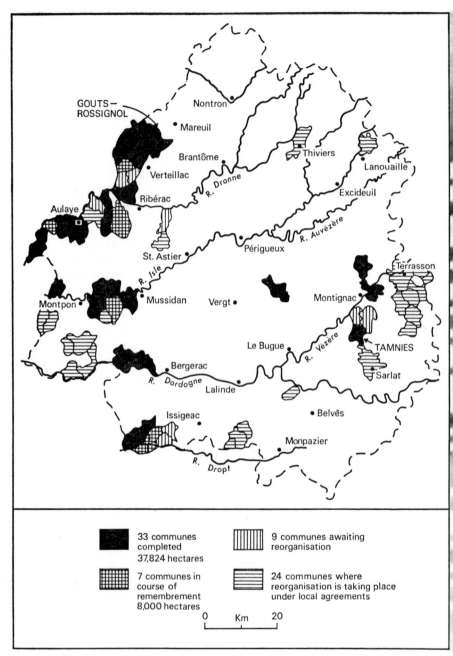

Fig 8 Remembrement: progress made to the end of 1973 (from information supplied by the Chambre d'Agriculture de la Dordogne)

efficient use of machinery and other forms of investment. Such specialisation may take the form of livestock in the Nontronnais and the Ribéracois, of fruit and market gardens in the principal river valleys, of vineyards in the Bergeracois, of tobacco in the Sarladais, of walnuts in the Lias basins and of strawberries in the forests of Vergt and Barade in central Périgord. Some crops, such as strawberries, are relatively new, but for the most part the emphasis is on a branch of what has long been a part of the polycultural tradition. Where better to begin a consideration of some of the more specialised forms of agriculture than with that strangest of all Périgord crops—the truffle.

### BLACK DIAMONDS

Truffles make the ladies loving and the gentlemen gallant.
Brillat Savarin

Known for centuries, Périgord truffles acquired their culinary reputation in the royal kitchens of eighteenth- and nineteenth-century Europe. Frederick the Great of Prussia was amongst those who appreciated the subtle flavour and aroma of 'le diamant noir' and he appointed a cook from Périgueux to ensure that its virtues were fully exploited in the dishes served to him. The production of truffles in Périgord reached a peak in the early years of the present century when between 100 and 150 tons a year were 'harvested' and sold through the markets of Périgueux, Sarlat, Thiviers or Excideuil. Truffle-culture collapsed, however, after World War I, and despite the continued demand from the luxury food industry, annual production of truffles from the whole of Périgord totalled no more than 3 tons during the 1960s. But thanks to the initiative of a number of individuals and to the work of the Syndicat des Producteurs de Truffes du Périgord which was set up in 1964, there are signs of a revival of this traditional agricultural activity, albeit now on a modern, scientific basis.

The truffle is a fungus—*Tuber Melanosporum*—black in colour and ranging in size from something no larger than an acorn to an object as big as one's fist and weighing perhaps half a kilo. Its surface is rough and convoluted and the fleshy interior is veined like marble, containing within it the minute spores from which the fungus develops. It grows on the roots of oaks, just below the surface of the earth, and the presence of truffles is usually indicated by a ring of 'burnt ground' which appears in the autumn above the place where the truffle will be found. If the truffle is very close to the surface its precise location within the ring may be revealed by a slight swelling and cracking of the soil just above it. Otherwise it has to be detected by other means and the time-honoured method is to employ a sow on some kind of lead. The sow has a natural taste for truffles and will find them from their aroma and by feeling the ground with its snout. The truffles can then be dug out with a metal-pointed tool. Dogs can also be trained to sniff them out and have the advantage of moving around faster, especially where there is brushwood or fallen branches lying about. On a calm winter's day a column of tiny, yellow flies will hover above a truffle leading, it is said, the skilled truffle-hunter to the spot where one may be found. He will mark it, taking care not to disturb the flies too much in case they settle over several places. How many hours must have been spent by amateurs looking for columns of yellow flies! For the expert there are many false alarms; equally, stories of surprise discoveries are legion. They are all part of the mystery and legend that has come to surround this curious object.

Truffle oaks grow best on limestone soils, ideally on *terra rossa*, reddish-brown soils resulting from the weathering *in situ* of the parent rock and its superficial deposits. The best conditions are found where the soil is underlain at no great depth by well-fissured limestone which results in good drainage but which prevents deep penetration of the roots, forcing them to spread out laterally. In Périgord truffle oaks are absent from the sandy

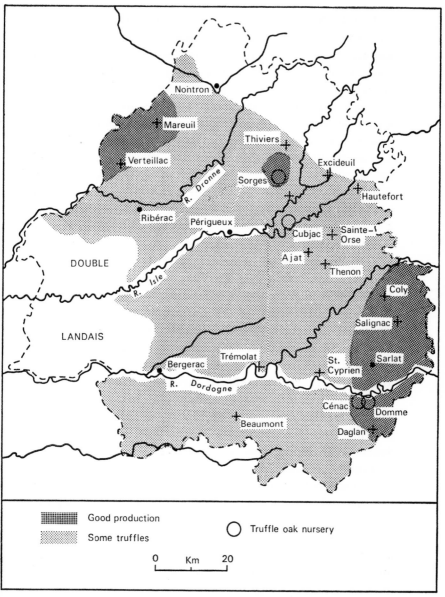

Fig 9  Distribution of the truffle (after **Léon Michel,** *Le Périgord: Le Pays et les Hommes*)

soils of the Nontronnais, the Double and the Landais, and from the alluvium of the major river valleys, but they occur widely elsewhere on both the Jurassic and the Cretaceous limestones, though they are associated most closely with the former. A high proportion of the truffles come, in fact, from the Causse and from the fringe of limestone plateau in the south-east which is an extension of the Causse de Quercy, ie around Coly, Salignac, Domme and Daglan. There is a scattered production from the extensive outcrop of Cretaceous rocks but the only locality comparable in importance with that of the Causse is a portion of the Ribéracois between Verteillac and Mareuil. Few truffles are found in central Périgord where the interfluves between the Isle and the Dordogne are widely covered with *sidérolithique* and Tertiary sands.

After the destruction of their vineyards by phylloxera, farmers who were not driven from the Causse turned to the collection and sale of truffles as a means of survival. New trees were planted and for thirty years or so the truffle-gathering economy flourished as never before. This brief period of prosperity ended with World War I. The trees were neglected during the war and became choked with the scrub vegetation of juniper, black-thorn, wild cherry and other bushes that spring up rapidly on the better soils of these limestone plateaux if they are not cleared regularly. Soil pests multiplied, so did the rabbits, and wartime losses of population meant that there was not the labour available to repair the damage.

Truffles are most likely to be found on the roots of oaks that have a stunted, even sickly appearance, but which is cause and which is effect is all a part of the mystery. The truffle begins its growth in spring, and rain at this time of year encourages the development of the spore. Rain in late summer, especially in August, is also good for swelling the fungus. As far as tempera-ture is concerned, truffles seem to mature best under conditions that are also well suited to the vine, but that is not to say they are absent where vines cannot easily be grown. Winter is the season for collecting them but the 'harvest' may be spread over all the months from October to March. It is an activity which fits in well with other demands on the farmer's time. Truffles, it is said, are more likely to form if the soil around the tree is lightened in the spring in order to aerate it, but nothing can be done to guarantee the appearance of truffles. Indeed their presence often seems to follow some kind of 'accident': the fall of a log, the passage over the ground of a heavy-wheeled cart, or even a brushwood fire.

Despite an obvious element of chance about truffle-culture, attempts have been made in recent years to increase production. Makers of pâté de foie gras and other foods in which they are used have been forced to buy their truffles outside Périgord, and there is no doubt that the demand from the luxury food trade is great enough to absorb a bigger local 'harvest'. Some planting of truffle oaks took place in the 1950s but with no success and it is only since 1964 and the formation of the Syndicat des Producteurs that progress has been made. With the encouragement of this organisation, young oaks are now being reared in nurseries and then planted out in specially prepared ground. Botanically there is no such thing as a truffle oak; it is simply an oak that happens to support truffles, and work in the laboratory has shown that oaks are most likely to do this if they are treated with mycelium, the substance from which the truffle is built up by the spores. It is possible to introduce mycelium to the roots of existing oaks but in the nurseries the acorns have it injected into them. Young trees are later planted out in ground that has been liberally treated with compost and here they are well spaced out, 6 to 10 metres apart, since plenty of light is essential if truffles are to form. This is likely to begin after about eight years, but growers are advised to let the first truffles decay in the ground in order to build up the presence of spores.

New plantations have been established in several parts of the Dordogne, but above all on the Causse where the efforts of a local agricultural adviser has encouraged farmers to look to the future. Pioneer work took place at Saint-Orse and at Coly, and the largest project so far is at Ajat near Thenon where 40 hectares of new oaks have been planted and another 60 hectares of oakwood cleared out and treated to induce truffle formation. The success of these ventures cannot yet be measured but it is an indication of changed attitudes to farming and land-use that the experiments have been made at all. Modern truffle-culture has little in common with the popular image of the old peasant woman following her sow through the woods on a still winter's day, yet this fungus, for so long an object of mystery, may still be capable of a few surprises.

# 6    LAND OF ALL GOOD THINGS

## TOBACCO

POLYCULTURE is most successful when it involves crops which demand a lot of personal attention; when time spent on tasks like weeding and pruning, and on careful harvesting, is more important than the use of machinery in large fields. Tobacco, a very time-consuming crop, is one which fits ideally into such a system. In addition, there is a guaranteed market and price assured by the government in the form of the Régie Nationale des Tabacs, so that the peasant grower can be sure of a cash reward for his efforts. At the same time, the acreage that is planted is strictly controlled by the Régie. Some idea of the scale of operations can be gained from the fact that, although there are more than 10,000 growers in Périgord, the total amount of land planted to tobacco is under 4,000 hectares, an average of under half a hectare (about one acre) each. A farmer with more than a hectare of land devoted to the crop is a grower on a big scale; most have only a few rows of plants.

A large proportion of the tobacco produced in Périgord comes from the Dordogne valley where the deep, rich alluvial soils are ideally suited to a crop which is as demanding of soil fertility as it is of labour. But a certain amount is also grown in the other river valleys and it is found fairly widely throughout the Sarladais in the *plaines* and on patches of easily worked sandy soil. In the Sarladais, tobacco was the crop which after the phylloxera attack helped to save the peasant farmer from ruin, just as the truffle was the salvation of his neighbours on the Causse. It is in these remoter spots that one is most likely to find the grower with just a row or two of plants; the larger holdings are in the main valley. The commercial centre for the tobacco grower is Bergerac. There is an Institut des Tabacs here which carries out research into methods and problems of cultivation, whilst information is also made available to growers from an organisation known as CIAP (Cercles d'Information Agricole des Planteurs). There is also a museum in Bergerac devoted to the history of tobacco.

Tobacco cultivation begins in the autumn with the careful preparation of the soil. This needs liberal applications of farm manure and it is said that dung from sheep gives the best results. Another way of ensuring soil fertility is to plant a leguminous 'culture dérobée' (literally: a hidden crop) and then plough it in when the ground is finally prepared in the spring. Mineral fertilisers are also employed when there is cash enough to spare for their purchase, but on the whole this is a crop which depends less on the availability of a large amount of capital than on a prodigal use of hand labour. The plants are raised in nursery beds, sometimes under glass, and are planted out in the open fields towards the end of May. Care is taken to space them out so that the individual plants catch the maximum sunlight and there is plenty of room for the leaves to develop. If they are spaced so that the leaves are just about touching at their maximum extent there will be less trouble from weeds because of the shade which the plants cast on the ground.

Rain in June after transplanting has taken place is ideal for rapid growth. Regular weeding is still necessary at this stage when the plants are small, and they also have to be earthed up. A second dressing of fertiliser may be applied and, as they develop, the poorer leaves closest to the ground are taken off so that the strength of the plant can go into a limited number of good leaves. For the same reason the flower stem is nipped out at a later stage. Sprays are used to deal with various kinds of

116

pests and diseases. All these operations demand labour and that is where the advantages of the peasant family lie, since there is work of some kind for all its members. Yet despite the care that is given to its cultivation, the crop can still be damaged by adverse weather. A summer that is too dry will result in leaves that are small and ill-formed, whereas too much rainfall will produce rank growth and a poor quality of leaf. Hail storms associated with summer thunderstorms can be as damaging to the tobacco crop as they are to the vineyards, battering the plants and tearing the leaves.

Harvesting the tobacco is another time-consuming operation and is likely to be spread over at least a month beginning in late August. Plants are cut individually, usually in the morning, and after they have wilted for an hour or two in the fields they are carried to the drying houses. These buildings, of brick or wood and roofed with tiles, are distinctive for the narrow, shuttered openings in the side which permit the air to circulate but keep out the direct rays of the sun. They can be seen in the villages or amongst the fields in the Dordogne valley, but not all growers possess a purpose-built drying house and on many small hold-ings tobacco plants can be seen hanging up to dry on wires inside the barn or some convenient farm shed. Needless to say, the quality of the finished product varies a good deal under such circumstances. The leaves take from forty to sixty days to dry and after that they are carefully stripped from the stalks, sorted according to size and quality and then bound in bundles of ten (*manoques*). These, in turn, are assembled in bales which by January or February are ready for despatch to one of the government depots (*centres de fermentation*) in Bergerac, Sarlat, Périgueux, Saint-Cyprien or Terrasson.

It has been estimated that the amount of labour absorbed by a single hectare of tobacco can be as high as 400 eight-hour days. Tobacco is also a plant that exhausts the soil and must be grown in rotation with grain and leguminous crops which restore some of the lost fertility. Yet it is popular because the

117

peasant farmer has found it to be one of his few secure sources of cash, and the income derived from it can enable necessary improvements to the home to be carried out. It has helped some families to survive on their smallholding and although the number of growers, as well as the cultivated acreage, is now tending to fall, this contraction is taking place at a time when the demand for other cash crops, notably vegetables and fruit, is rising.

### WALNUTS

More than any other tree, the walnut is both an integral part of the landscape of Périgord and an essential element in the peasant economy. Its thick, green foliage throws into relief the grey cliffs bordering the river valleys and, scattered amongst the fields, individual trees break up the geometrical shapes of the farm plots. Its nuts are a useful addition to the cash income of the small farmer; it provides oil for salads and cooking, and when the trees are too old to bear they are cut down and used to make those magnificent pieces of farmhouse furniture that serve generation after generation of families.

Walnut oil was already being exported from Périgord in the seventeenth century. At that time the principal markets were in England and Holland and the oil that was produced, mostly from trees growing in the Dordogne valley and the Sarladais, was shipped through Bordeaux. From the middle of the nineteenth century the export trade grew as the sale of nuts was added to that of oil, again under the stimulus of merchants in Bordeaux, and the walnut spread to the Causse and to the Lias basins which fringe the Causse to the east. Hard-shelled varieties were grown here which stood up better to the rigours of transport than the soft-shelled nuts of the Sarladais. In this latter district a trade in shelled kernels grew up alongside the older one in oil.

Following the agricultural crisis of the 1870s, the popularity of walnuts increased and *le noyer*, like the truffle oak, was a means of survival for smallholders whose vines had been destroyed by phylloxera. New plantings took place on the Causse and in the bordering basins, but in the Sarladais there was greater emphasis on tobacco and other field crops. During the present century there has been little new planting except for replacement—and that only erratically—but in recent years some attempts have been made to establish plantations of trees that can be managed on scientific lines. Examples can be found at Saint-Georges-de-Montclar in the Bergeracois and at Doissat in the Pays de Belvès where nearly a hundred hectares of woodland were cleared and more than 7,000 walnut trees planted. In this way the walnut, like the truffle oak, is submitting to the modern ideas that are beginning to permeate the agriculture of the region. There is now a co-operative organisation that supplies young trees to planters, and a body known as the Comité Interprofessionnel de la Noix et du Noyer is active in the dissemination of ideas. Despite the influence of such organisations, however, the culture of the walnut remains for the most part very traditional.

Dordogne is the leading département in France for the production of walnuts with an annual harvest of 6,000 to 8,000 tons, and the sale of nuts contributes to the income of some 12,000 farmers. The walnut has an unusually short vegetative season; its leaves appear late after the last of the spring frosts and they are shed early. In order to yield a good crop of nuts it needs heavy rain in spring and a certain amount of rainfall through the summer with, ideally, a dry spell at the end of summer when the nuts are reaching maturity. On the whole the climatic conditions in Périgord are well suited to these demands, though the occasional dry summer may result in nuts that are late or ill-formed. If it is very wet the nuts do not ripen well and tend to fall early. They are also prone to fungus diseases.

The tree likes a deep soil that is well drained but not too permeable. Optimum conditions are to be found on the clay-marls of the Lias basins and it is here, in the vicinity of Thiviers,

Excideuil, Cubas and La Bachellerie, that the greatest density of trees is to be found. But they also do well on the limestone, favouring valley slopes, combes where there has been an accumulation of eroded material, and the patches of *terra rossa* on the plateau above. Walnuts are common on these more favoured parts of the Causse, with a high concentration in the neighbourhood of Sorges and Negrondes, but they are also found scattered over the outcrop of Cretaceous limestones, avoiding only the hill cappings of sand and gravel. Walnuts are rare in the Nontronnais and on the Tertiary rocks of the Double, the Landais and the Bergeracois, although there has been some recent planting even here.

A casual observer will see very little pattern or order in the distribution of walnut trees. They are dotted about amongst the farm plots apparently at random; they appear in clusters or as single trees at the bottom of the garden, and they sometimes line the tracks or minor roads that lead from the village to the fields. Yet each has its owner and a single farmer may possess just two or three trees and indeed may have a part share in only one of them. There are very few specialist growers and for most farmers the walnut is no more than a useful sideline, providing a supplement to his cash income. The trees are valued greatly nevertheless. New ones are planted from time to time, the best-yielding varieties being those that have been grafted on to American root stock, but it is about fifteen years before the tree bears a crop of nuts and twenty before it is mature. Scattered haphazardly about and at varying stages of maturity, it is hardly surprising that walnuts make the reallocation of land holdings so difficult.

The nuts ripen towards the end of September. In some parts of France they are picked from the trees, but in the Dordogne they are generally allowed to fall and it tends to be the work of the women or children to gather them—in the morning before they are crushed by carts, or before farm animals have got at them. A few are kept back for eating on the farm; some go to the mill where oil is extracted, but most are sold, the big demand coming at Christmas. West Germany provides the biggest market for the hard-shelled nuts, kernels from the softer-shelled varieties coming principally to Britain. Before the kernels can be exported they must be shelled and this, too, is women's work, often left to the grandmother or some other elderly relative who sits at her door with a basket of nuts breaking them on a board with a wooden hammer. Needless to say the *énoisement* becomes something of a social occasion.

There are few plants from which the French farmer cannot make some kind of palatable drink and the walnut is no exception to the rule. Its leaves are made into the apéritif, quinquina, and the husks can be crushed and blended with a little eau-de-vie to make *crème de noix*, a rich black liqueur with more than a hint of liquorice about it. One begins to understand why Philip Oyler described the Dordogne as 'the land of all good things'.

### STRAWBERRIES

Quite the most remarkable transformation in the agriculture of Périgord has taken place in what at first seems the most unlikely part of the region, the wooded uplands between the valleys of the Isle and the Dordogne to the south of Périgueux. Here, amongst the chestnut woods of the Forêt de Vergt and around Rouffignac on the edge of the Forêt Barade, strawberry-growing has brought about a transformation in the peasant way of life over the course of the last twenty years.

It is a success story that began in the late 1940s when a few pioneers gave up traditional forms of cereal cultivation to concentrate on fruit, vegetables and also milk for the urban market. This took place in the villages immediately to the south of Périgueux—Atur, Notre-Dame-de-Sanilhac, Marsaneix and Eglise-Neuve—from which the goods could be taken easily to the town market. Strawberries were found to do particularly well on the sandy soils which cap the upper slopes and other farmers were encouraged to copy the pioneers. The sandy deposits are more extensive on the wooded interfluves to the south of the original nucleus of cultivation and so the crop spread southwards during the 1950s to Villamblard and Vergt and eastwards to Rouffignac and to Montignac in the valley of the Vézère. In these parts, agriculture had been largely confined to the lower slopes of dry valleys dissecting the uplands. Here in the valley bottoms there was sufficient depth of downwash material to support patches of cereals but the slopes above were left to chestnut forest. Now the forests were grubbed up using bulldozers and the clearings gradually enlarged.

By the late 1950s the new crop was sufficiently well established to enable the growers to experiment with new varieties of plant brought in from elsewhere. Ones were found that were less subject to virus diseases than the original strains and efforts were made to grow strawberries of a better size and flavour. In 1959 the first co-operative was opened to market the crop with its depot at Les Bitarelles on the main road from Périgueux to Bergerac. The strawberries are graded and packed at the depot and sent off daily during the season by lorry to Paris and other cities.

The spread of strawberry cultivation in Périgord provides a remarkably good example of agricultural innovation and diffusion. From its core area near Périgueux, the crop had been widely adopted by 1960 in the uplands to the south. Since that time it has been taken up in other parts of the region, notably around Trémolat below the confluence of the Dordogne and the Vézère, in the Nontronnais where Augignac is at the centre of a strawberry-growing district, and west of Périgueux on the low hills between the valleys of the Isle and the Dronne. As in all histories of diffusion, attempts have constantly been made to improve the quality of the crop by adopting new varieties and improving methods of cultivation and marketing. Latterly these efforts have been aimed at producing early varieties that catch the most lucrative market, and a small proportion of the

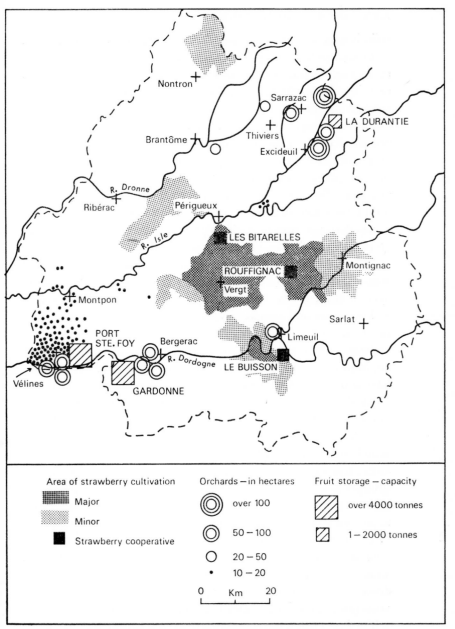

Fig 10 Strawberries and orchard fruits (after René Pijassou, *Regards sur la Révolution Agricole en Dordogne*)

crop is now grown under plastic cloches and even under glass.

There are four co-operative depots now that handle between them about a third of the total strawberry crop, guaranteeing a certain price to the grower; the remainder are sold through the more traditional market organisations several of which have their headquarters in Vergt. In addition to the original co-operative depot of Les Bitarelles there are others at Rouffignac, at Port-Sainte-Foy (a big co-operative in the Dordogne valley that handles other kinds of fruit as well—page 128), and a small one at Le Buisson to serve the Vézère/Dordogne area. By 1970 total production of strawberries from the whole of Périgord had reached 10,000 tons or 15 per cent of the national figure. Some 30 per cent of the crop is exported, mainly to Britain, Germany and Switzerland. Rail facilities, which include refrigerated wagons, are used for despatching strawberries to their more distant markets and special handling depots have been set up at Périgueux and also at Niversac which, like Le Buisson, is a junction on the main line.

Strawberries have been successful in Périgord because they are well suited to the natural environment and because they have fitted in well to the established pattern of peasant farming. They do best on light, permeable, lime-free soils with a good humus content and almost ideal conditions are to be found on the sandy, wooded hills of central Périgord. The climate is sufficiently humid in the early summer to encourage a good formation of fruit and warm, damp weather at the end of summer is beneficial to next year's growth. Since the plants are generally grown on slopes rather than valley bottoms, they avoid the danger of late spring frosts. The chestnut woodlands of the Forêt de Vergt and elsewhere constituted a reserve of land which the strawberry growers have been able to exploit. This has been important because the plant is prone to virus diseases if it is grown for more than about four years on the same plot, and it is necessary to move on constantly to new land.

The best crop is harvested in the second season and the plants are frequently uprooted after their third summer. Land is then freed for other crops—roots, potatoes, maize, small grains or legumes—and so the growing of strawberries brings about indirectly an extension of these other crops and an improvement in the general quality of the farming as a whole. This has certainly been the case in those parts of Périgord where strawberries have been adopted. Farm income has risen; there has been money to improve the home; the drift from the land has been checked and there are instances of younger members of the family who had left, coming back and setting up as growers, even building themselves new houses. The pioneers have been fortunate, of course, in the sense that there has been plenty of forest land to clear and fresh soil always available. If the demand increases, this advantage will inevitably disappear, and it is to offset the problems that could arise when there is less 'virgin territory' that growers are experimenting with methods of growing strawberries for a more continuous period on the same land. One such method is to protect the plants from too much contact with the soil by allowing them to grow through holes made in long sheets of black plastic material which are spread over the field. Meanwhile forest clearance continues and sale of the timber pays the cost of hiring equipment for uprooting it. Chestnut wood can be sent to the factory at Montignac where rustic furniture, boxes for the fruit and a range of other articles are made.

There are at present about 2,000 strawberry growers in Périgord with an average of a half to two-thirds of a hectare each under the crop—yields may be as high as 12 tons to the hectare. A lot of work is involved but again it is of a kind that can be shared by the whole family, a fact that, together with the quick returns obtained, helps to explain the readiness with which the crop has been adopted in the region. The greatest demand for labour comes about the middle of May when picking begins and lasts until the end of June. Extra pickers have to be employed and they are recruited locally on a temporary basis. Many of them are women and the total employed at any one time can be as high as 10,000. Some varieties of strawberry also yield a second harvest at the end of August, if they have been irrigated, but the need for extra labour at this time of year is very much less than in early summer.

Over the course of time, the boundary of the forest in Périgord has fluctuated in response to a variety of pressures, economic, social and political. It constitutes one of the most interesting aspects of the region's history. Peace and population growth has brought with it forest clearance as happened, for example, in the twelfth and thirteenth centuries or in the early nineteenth century. At other times the forest has gained at the expense of the cultivated land and this has generally been true of the last hundred years following the agricultural crisis of the 1870s and the resultant loss of population. To the hopefully minded, the *défrichement* associated with the growing of strawberries is seen as the start of a new phase of clearance, part of a general revival in the agriculture of the whole region. Such a view may be over-optimistic, or at least premature. Nevertheless in those parts of the region where the new form of agriculture has been introduced there is a sense of purpose and an appearance of prosperity that gives rise to hope.

### ORCHARD FRUITS

Few parts of the Dordogne region are without a scattering of fruit trees yielding apples, pears, peaches or plums. They are a part of the tradition of 'un peu de tout'. Since the late 1950s, however, attempts have been made to put fruit-growing on a more commercial basis and these efforts have been notably successful in two areas: the crystalline uplands of the north where large quantities of apples are now grown, and in the Dordogne valley below Bergerac where peaches are the main crop but other fruits are also produced.

Extensive new apple orchards are now reaching maturity on

the hillsides beyond Thiviers and Excideuil in the vicinity of such places as Saint-Médard, Lanouaille, Sarrazac, Sarlande and Miallet. They do well on the acid soils derived from schist and gneiss, and the climatic conditions of these uplands, cooler and more humid than elsewhere in Périgord, are also well suited to apples. Hill slopes are preferred in order to reduce the frost risk but it is still necessary to use orchard heaters occasionally in the spring.

The popularity of apple orchards in this part of the Dordogne owes something to the proximity of the town of Brive, an established fruit-growing area, but credit must also be given, as in the case of strawberries, to the enterprise of a few individuals. A good example is to be seen at La Durantie near Lanouaille where this estate, famous for the improving work of Marshal Bugeaud in the nineteenth century, has more recently been the scene of pioneer work in fruit production. Since 1965 apples grown here have been sold under the trade name of 'Vergers du Père Bugeaud'. Other estate owners, like Madame André Maurois at Essendiéras, have similarly converted what was often poor scrub or grassland to orchards and the practice of creating small artificial lakes—once used in connection with the iron industry—has been revived to provide a supply of irrigation water. Seasonal labour, mostly Spanish or Portuguese, is employed to pick the fruit, and a refrigerated depot has been built close to the railway station at Excideuil where the despatch of apples is organised. Most are exported, but overproduction in the Common Market has posed certain problems in the last few years which some see as a threat to the newfound prosperity.

In the Dordogne valley there are extensive peach groves around Castang and Gardonne and also between Port-Sainte-Foy and Vélines. Peaches yield best on light, well-drained soils like the *boulbènes* of the river terraces. They also benefit from irrigation so that proximity to the river is an advantage. Latterly, however, as the distribution of water has improved, peach orchards have spread north of the river over the low, sandy ridges of the Landais towards Montpon and Mussidan in the valley of the Isle to the north. Commercial production of peaches began in a small way near Bergerac in the 1930s and this early venture has grown into a large organisation with its depot for sorting, grading and packing at Gardonne.

Planting of orchards lower down the valley has taken place more recently, mainly since 1956 when the disastrous frosts of that winter destroyed vineyards and other fruit trees (the temperature in February fell as low as $-25°$ C). A major role in this transformation has been played by the co-operative known as Valcodor (Vallée-Coteaux-Dordogne) which began operations at Port-Sainte-Foy in 1960. It is the largest organisation of its kind in Périgord and handles not only peaches but also apples, plums, strawberries and even walnuts. To it comes fruit from small family farms with no more than a hectare of trees and from large specialised orchard holdings with a hundred hectares or more, and to all the growers who belong to it, it affords a degree of financial security that goes a long way to explaining the rapid spread of orchards in this south-western corner of Périgord. Forest clearance for strawberries in the Forêt de Vergt and elsewhere is closely paralleled by what is now happening in the Landais, where small hedged fields and scrub woodland are giving way to plantations of fruit trees and the effect on the local agricultural community has been equally beneficial.

The Valcodor co-operative operates throughout the year, having extensive cold storage facilities which permits the sale of fruit to be adjusted to market demand. Fresh fruit can be bought there in season but most of it is despatched by road or rail, the depot being situated alongside both the main road, N136, and the railway to Bordeaux. Exports are mostly to northern European countries but consignments have been sent to Latin America. Peaches and apples are supplied to a supermarket chain in Britain.

Other parts of Périgord have shared less in the commercialisation of fruit-growing than the two areas just described, but here and there it is possible to see orchards that have been newly planted. They are most in evidence around the confluence of the Vézère and the Dordogne at Limeuil, but there is a sprinkling of them along the Isle valley, including some pear orchards, and in that of its tributary, the Auvézère near Le Change. South of Périgueux there is a new fruit-growing district around Grun and Bourron in the basin of the river Vergt which boasts locally of being 'une Californie périgordine'. Several such plantations are the work of repatriates from North Africa who have settled in Périgord and acquired properties. In the extreme south of the region, the area around Eymet in the valley of the Dropt sees an extension of the plum-growing industry of the Agenais.

## LIVESTOCK

Under a system of polyculture, livestock are of secondary importance to field and tree crops; they are kept to satisfy the requirements of the family in meat and milk, but livestock products enter to only a small extent, if at all, into cash sales. Such a system has prevailed over much of Périgord, although a certain amount of cash was forthcoming from the sale of 'small animals', especially geese but also rabbits and ducks, and the honey collected from a few hives of bees. More recently a small quantity of milk may also have entered into farm sales. Exceptions to this rule, however, are encountered in the northern parts of the region where, in the Ribéracois and the Nontronnais, livestock occupy a much more prominent position in the farm economy. Concern for livestock is not entirely new in these parts, but there has been an increase in production, particularly of veal and lamb, coupled with greater attention to stock breeding and to the growing of feed crops. The revival in agriculture associated with the changes has been comparable in its impact on the local community with that associated with fruit-growing elsewhere in the region.

On the farms of the Ribéracois there is a dual emphasis on the production of wheat and veal (*veau blanc*). The district has a reputation for both of these that was noted as long ago as the early nineteenth century by the agricultural reformer, the Marquis de Fayolle, but specialisation increased after 1870 when the vineyards were destroyed by phylloxera. Wheat yields well on the chalky soils and it is grown in rotation with maize and other small grains and with feed crops, including sainfoin, trefoil and temporary grasses. Improved varieties of wheat have been tried out in recent years and good bread grains are produced that are popular with bakers. There are grain storage depots at Ribérac, Verteillac and Rossignol.

Calves for veal are raised on the farm and sold at the age of three to four months when their average weight has reached 150 kilograms. The practice of bringing in breeding stock from outside the region is long-established and Limousin has always been the principal source of supply. Since most of the farms are small—the average herd has fewer than ten cows—and capital is correspondingly limited, it is not uncommon to find that the breeding stock is not, in fact, owned by the farmer but is loaned by firms of stock merchants who share the profits from the sale of calves with the farmers. It is a form of 'sharecropping' known as *attelle* and frees the farmer from the problem of disposing of his unwanted breeding stock. The latter are taken by the stock merchants, some of whom also have interests in the butchery trade.

*Veau blanc* is known also as *Veau de Chalais* from the name of the leading market which is just outside Périgord in the département of Charente. The calves are fed almost exclusively on milk, but their diet also includes such exotic extras as sugar and the whites of eggs. In this way the meat acquires its whiteness and its reputation; grain-fed veal is less highly valued. There is some surplus production of milk and cream, most of which finds its way to the dairy co-operatives in neighbouring Charente, but a number of dairies have been established in the Ribéra-cois itself. A move towards this was initiated in the 1920s when the immigrant farm workers from Brittany and Vendée were settled in the region. Whey is fed to pigs on the farm.

Success with veal has encouraged some farmers to extend their interests to include the sale of lambs as well. Those known as *agneaux blancs* are raised in a very similar way to the calves, wholly under cover and fed largely on ewes' milk and a certain amount of meal. Sold as '100-day' lambs, they are intended largely for the Christmas market. Other lambs, born in the spring and allowed to feed on grass, are sold towards the end of summer at the age of four to five months. There are a number of specialist farms, mostly large enterprises, but in general the production of lamb occupies a secondary place to that of veal.

Sheep are rare in the Nontronnais but there is a varied live-stock industry in this part of the Dordogne region based mainly on cattle and pigs. Improved rotations with more emphasis on feed crops and temporary pastures, together with improved breeding, have done much to advance the industry. The supply of piped water, here as well as in the Ribéracois, has also helped. Dairy herds are common but milk production takes second place to that of beef and veal, and milk-fed veal is important here also. It is sold as *Veau de Lyon* or *Veau de Saint-Etienne* and fairs for the sale of veal calves are held at Chalus and Saint-Yrieix in neighbouring Limousin. Some farms specialise in pigs which are sold as porklets at about two months, or are kept for between one and two years when they can be sold as fat pigs. Piégut is an important centre. Potatoes are widely grown, both for feeding to pigs and for sale.

It is likely that livestock numbers will continue to grow in the Dordogne region as the demand for meat increases both within France and in the Common Market as a whole. There are signs of the changes that rising demand can bring about even in such unpromising environments as the Double where here and there woodland and heath is giving way to pasture. Not far from Bergerac the Coopérative d'Insémination Artificielle maintains something like thirty pedigree bulls and the centre has contributed enormously towards improving the quality of the region's cattle. Nothing could be further removed from the old pattern of farming.

# 7        A FRIGHTFUL COUNTRY

THE forests of Périgord have not always left a favourable impression on the mind of the traveller. To the Chevalier de Lagrange-Chancel, the Double in the eighteenth century was a 'pays affreux', a frightful country that was only good for hunting wild beasts. Even the peasants described the wooded hills as 'the black country' (the *pays negré*), a place of retreat when war or plague threatened. And stories are still told of old men discovered living in the forest who had not left their small holdings in a quarter of a century.

Yet the forest is an integral part of the life and landscape of the Dordogne, accounting for between a quarter and a third of the total area. Dark, forested hilltops are an essential backdrop to the airy, well-cultivated valleys, and despite its reputation, the woodland has been of considerable value to man; indeed the history of the region cannot be understood without reference to it. It has been a source of food and fuel as well as of materials for building and industry. Indeed, as we have seen, it has acted as a measure of the economic health of the region, the forest edge retreating as population has increased or as new crops have been introduced, advancing as circumstances have caused farmland to be abandoned. It has provided sport, and the wolf features prominently in regional folklore. The forest has been a sanctuary to monks and priests, and it has served as a frontier, separating rival factions whose main interest has been in the towns and the rich land of the valleys. During the struggles between different parties it has acted not only as a hiding place but as a centre of resistance to whatever system outsiders were seeking to impose. Stragglers from defeated armies would often retreat to the forest only to encounter a peasantry hostile and resentful because their property had been looted or destroyed, and not all emerged alive. As recently as World War II the forests of Périgord acted as a centre of resistance to German occupation.

CHESTNUT WOODS

The woodland flora of Périgord is a very mixed one, betraying climatic conditions that are in many respects transitional between the Mediterranean and northern Europe, as well as between coast and interior. The beech, for example, extends as far south as Périgord, encountering the Montpellier maple and evergreen oak from Languedoc, whilst western maritime species are represented by the black oak and gorse. To these climatic influences must be added environmental contrasts that occur within the region as a result of differences between upland and valley, limestone and sands. On the Causse the most typical association is of white oak with hornbeam and juniper scrub, whereas chestnuts and pines dominate the outcrops of ferruginous sands. There is an undergrowth of bracken, gorse and broom with tangled ivy and brambles. The rivers are bordered by willows and alder and, in places especially in the Sarladais, by rows of Lombardy poplar. Above them, ferns, mosses and climbing plants add a splash of colour to the grey rocky outcrops on the valley sides.

In spite of the varied nature of the flora, the forests appear to the casual observer to be dominated by three trees: oak, chestnut and pine. Oaks are the most common and almost all species of oak are represented, but it is the chestnut that contributes most to the character of the woodlands. No other part of France except Corsica has such a wealth of chestnut forest and it is the presence of the chestnut with its brightly coloured flowers and its distinctive long, pointed leaves that at once strikes the visitor. The Dordogne has been described as the 'pays du châtaignier'. Both oak and pine have several uses, but it is the chestnut that has sustained life when crops have failed, contributing also to the importance of the region as a home for early man.

The sweet chestnut needs a warm climate and can tolerate a measure of summer drought; it cannot stand cold, humid conditions. The climate of Périgord is well suited to its requirements. It also likes an acid, siliceous soil and is therefore most common in the Double and the Landais, the Nontronnais, and on the ferruginous sands that cap the hills so extensively in Central Périgord and the Sarladais. Here in the Forêt de Chancelade, the Forêt Barade or the Forêt de Belvès, it is seen in its most typical setting. In places the woodland is almost exclusively composed of chestnuts, frequently coppiced; elsewhere the trees occur in clumps or simply scattered amongst the oak woodland. Formal clustering of trees usually denotes an old plantation, established in order to harvest the nuts more easily. Trees that were grown for their nuts are confined, for the most part, to the central and eastern parts of the region where they thrive best. Chestnuts in the Double and the Landais tend to have a more stunted growth, except on well-drained slopes, because of the presence near the surface of water held up by the impervious layer of clay. Here the trees are almost all coppiced, yielding wood for various purposes, rather than commercial quantities of nuts.

It is necessary to write about the chestnut woods to some extent in the past tense because their commercial importance has changed with time. They are still a valuable source of timber, but they no longer provide a staple food and the demand for charcoal and tannin is now only a small one. Until as late as the present century, however, the chestnut was *l'arbre vital* to the peasant and each holding would have its patch of chestnut wood, even if it were at some distance from the main property. Until potatoes came to be widely grown, the chestnut was a staple food—the *aliment de base*—in the peasant diet, as well as feed for the pig. Provided they were properly dried in the sun to prevent them going bad, the nuts could be kept through the winter, and even in the nineteenth century when potatoes were common, the chestnut was an essential standby if other crops failed. Nuts were also exported and there is evidence of a trade in chestnuts in the Sarladais from the fourteenth century. Like the walnuts, they were loaded in sacks on to boats and sent down the Dordogne to Bordeaux.

Like walnuts also, the best fruiting varieties of chestnut were grafted and the trees reached maturity and were fully bearing after about twenty-five years. The nuts ripen at the end of September and in early October, and they were picked as they fell or knocked from the trees with sticks. Nothing was wasted; husks and leaves were gathered and used as fertiliser on the potato patch much as farmers in the west of Ireland spread sea-weed on their *lazy beds*. When the trees were too old to bear, they were cut down and sold for timber, even the shavings being used for the extraction of tannin. Factories for this purpose were set up at Couze in the Dordogne valley in 1899 and at Condat near Terrasson in 1907.

Coppiced chestnuts grow rapidly and after five to eight years their smooth, silvery shoots can be chopped down and cut into thin strips for making barrel hoops, rustic furniture or garden lattice. A year or two later the growth is sturdy enough to yield stakes for sale to the vine-growers (*carassones*) and for a long time there has been a ready market for these in the Bordelais and elsewhere. From about fifteen years, the trees are used in the joinery industry. Chestnut wood has the great virtue of resisting rainwater which makes it a popular material for doors, shutters and window-frames, as well as for garden furniture. Pit props were once exported but the need for these has fallen with the decline of coalmining; by contrast the demand for rustic furniture is increasing and is likely to continue to do so as more properties are converted into holiday cottages. Chestnut wood is also used for domestic heating and

*Page 137*
Saint-Amand-de-
Coly and its
fortified church

Page 138 (above) Abbey church
and bell tower at Brantôme;
(left) fortified church at
Beaumont-du-Périgord

as a source of charcoal, but it has never been as highly valued as oak for these purposes, since the wood creates a lot of sparks as it burns and a domestic fire needs to be watched rather carefully.

It was once a custom in Périgord for the family to assemble in the kitchen before the evening meal was served when a row of roasted chestnuts was laid across the kitchen table. The head of the household would eat one or two, followed by all the other members of the family, after which they would begin their dinner. It was a kind of thanksgiving that reminded everyone of the importance once attached to the chestnut in the traditional diet.

Times have changed and the chestnut is no longer valued by the ordinary family as once it was. Population loss in the late nineteenth century resulted in the neglect of the chestnut plantations and some of the trees became diseased. One of the most common is a disease known as *l'encre* from the inky-black substance that is exuded by the tree. In places the chestnut woods are now being cut down to make way for more profitable forms of land-use such as strawberries. But this is not to say that the chestnut no longer has an ecological role to play. The wooded areas can be looked upon as a reserve of potential farmland, the trees building up humus and fertility in the acid, sandy soils. The woods also harbour game, and when they are cut the trees are a source of cash that helps to pay for the agricultural improvements. Latterly there has even been some replacement of the native chestnuts with a Japanese variety which is resistant to the *encre* and which gives a tasty chestnut valued by the confectioners who make marrons glacés.

## THE DOUBLE

Not a sign of life in the gloomy landscape except for a flight of wood-pigeons above the tree-tops. Sickening odours rose from the marshes of this wretched land, shrouded in a cold and penetrating damp. An inexpressible melancholy hung over this desolate region, the ancient *Sylva Edobola* where the freedom of Aquitaine was finally lost with the death of Waïfer her last sovereign duke, and what was once a proud 'Land of Conquest' has become the realm of fever.

*L'Ennemi de la Mort*

There is still an atmosphere of solitude and mystery about the Double in spite of the motor cars on its roads and the pleasure boats on the Grand Etang. Three-quarters of the land in the heart of the Double is under forest and it is possible to walk long distances through woodland unbroken except for the occasional clearing or small lake. It has always been a poor country—'un mauvais pays'—and the sufferings of the peasantry have been immortalised in Eugène Le Roy's novel *L'Ennemi de la Mort* (1913) which he wrote at the end of the last century. It describes the work of a doctor whose life was devoted to combating the disease and poverty that made this such a *pays affreux*. In part the problems were overcome by emigration and the Double is today one of the most sparsely populated parts of the Dordogne if not of France as a whole. Like all forested areas it has its 'moods' which are closely related to the prevailing weather conditions, but on a calm summer's evening the play of sunlight on trees and *étangs*, makes it one of the most enchanting parts of the whole of Périgord.

The Double is a country of low hills and ridges between the valleys of the Isle and the Dronne, delimited very approximately to the east by the main road from Mussidan to Ribérac. Its undulating skyline is broken by a few heights like the Signal d'Echourgnac (133 metres), which owe their resistance to bands of harder rock, and below the ridges are gently sloping hollows from which streams flow in surprisingly deep and narrow valleys (Chapter 2). Small lakes occupy them, strung out in places like a row of beads along the valley. Most are small, only the Etang de la Jemaye—the Grand Etang—being of any appreciable size, 33 hectares. The Domaine de la Jemaye was purchased by the state before the last war and has been developed for water sports, fishing and as a centre for forest research.

It is likely that many of the lakes are man-made, although they no doubt correspond with naturally marshy tracts. During the Middle Ages lakes were created by building simple dams across the valleys and they became a valuable source of fish, especially important to the nearby monasteries like that of Vauclaire. There are still about a hundred lakes in the Double, but old maps show more than this, some of them having been drained during the nineteenth century when the first attempts were being made to eradicate mosquitoes.

The Double is closer to the sea than any other part of Périgord. This, and its forest cover, serve to moderate extremes of temperature but they also give it a reputation for being damp and miasmal. Humidity is increased by the lakes, and at night fogs often form in the valleys where they can linger well into the day. In a rainy spell the whole landscape seems to run or drip with water and the sandy soil is washed across the roads. But there are also dry periods, and it was at such times that the lakes used to become little more than stagnant pools, classic breeding grounds for mosquitoes. Disease in consequence was rife, and deaths from *le fièvre* were common until well into the second half of the last century. A report was published on the problem in 1863 and figures in the report show that, for example, the commune of Echourgnac experienced 1,194 live births between 1803 and 1850, but in the same period recorded 1,350 deaths. Echourgnac is in the middle of the Double, with many lakes nearby, but mortality was high almost everywhere. After the report appeared efforts began to be made to control disease; some lakes were drained and others were embanked to maintain a greater depth of water. Streams were also cleared of the fallen trees, silt and other debris that had accumulated in them and reduced their flow.

Soils in the Double are podsolised and acid, naturally infer-

tile and requiring liberal applications of lime and other fertilisers if they are to be cultivated. They are mostly derived from
sands or clays, exceptions occurring where there is an outcrop
of *grisou*, a yellowish conglomerate which in the past has provided a useful building material. It can be seen used in the walls
of the interesting old church at Saint-André-de-Double.

Because of its poor soils the Double has always been well
forested—witness its old name of Sylva Edobola. The oak is the
most common tree, both the pedunculate variety—the white
oak—which provides good timber for the carpenter—and also
the black oak (*chêne tauzin*) with its characteristic ribbed bark,
used mainly for fuel and charcoal. The black oak seems to
thrive particularly well here and so much was sold at one time
that it was known as 'charbon du Périgord'.

Other trees include the chestnut, valued mainly for its timber
rather than its fruit, the maritime pine, the hornbeam which
prefers the deeper soil of the valleys, and less commonly, birch,
willow, aspen, acacia and even lime. Maritime pine was regarded as an unwelcome intruder in the forest until the late
nineteenth century when the success of plantings in the Landes
persuaded local landowners to encourage it. New plantations
were made, but the pine is self-regenerating and spread rapidly.
It has a long root that breaks through the hardpan and improves
the natural drainage so that planting with pines assisted the
work of draining lakes and marshes. The trees afforded timber
for pit props and construction but they were mostly valued for
their resin which was collected in little cups fastened to the tree
below an incision made in the bark. Resin is still obtained in
this way but the practice is dying out, most turpentine now
coming as a by-product of pulp and paper manufacture in the
Landes and elsewhere.

There is extensive heath and scrub in the Double as well as
mature woodland. Gorse, broom and heather grow vigorously,
their stems strong enough to break the blade of a scythe.
Bracken is plentiful and in the last century it was collected in

large quantities for stable litter and sent by the cartload to the farms of more favoured areas nearby. It was sold in the open market at Montpon and Mussidan. Many farms outside the Double did, in fact, own land here which they exploited for its timber and litter. Even on the farms that lay wholly within the Double, well over half the holding usually consisted of woodland or heath and it was this that provided the small amount of cash income that the peasant farmer earned. Wood was cut during the winter; this was also the season for hunting game, so there was plenty of work throughout the year. There were dangers though, from wolves and wild boar and also from snakes, especially vipers for which the Double was once notorious. The lakes were, and still are, a valuable source of fish. It was common practice to drain one of the *étangs* every few years and the villagers would then collect the fish from the mud and carry them in their straw-lined baskets to market. There was always a good sale for fish at Easter and the occasion of emptying the lakes was both something of a ceremony (*petitone*) and an excuse for merrymaking.

Farms are generally well scattered in the Double, seeking out sites on better-drained ground where a patch of woodland can be cleared for cultivation. Their long, low buildings were once of wood, but now are more commonly of locally-made brick and tile or of blocks of *grisou*. Staple crops were rye for bread, millet or maize which was made into a kind of dumpling (*mique*), potatoes—with asparagus one of the few crops that does well in the Double—and a row or two of vines. After publication of the *Rapport sur la Double* in 1863, however, serious attempts were made to improve the lot of the impoverished peasantry and to open up the region. New roads were built which facilitated the export of forest products; they also enabled agricultural lime to be brought in to improve the quality of the soil. Quarries at Saint-Astier were the main source of lime, and stone for road-building was brought down the Isle in flat-bottomed boats from Excideuil. The Isle had been improved for navigation in 1815 and could accommodate 50 to 80 ton boats known as *coureaux*. Further works were carried out on the river in the 1830s.

In 1864 an agricultural advisory service was established at Echourgnac. Farmers were taught to grow leguminous crops, roots and ley grasses and there was a gradual shift towards cattle farming with the emphasis on milk production. A lead was given by the monks of a Trappist monastery that had been founded near Echourgnac—the Trappe de Bonne Espérance. Like Marshal Bugeaud's estate in the Nontronnais, the monastery was a centre of agricultural innovation from which ideas spread through the surrounding farm community. The monks collected milk from the peasants and made it into cheese. Happily, cheeses can still be bought at the gates of the monastery. To the monks must also be given credit for taking medical knowledge to the peasant homes. In the early years they would always carry quinine with them. But the dangers of malaria were gradually reduced as the marshy tracts were drained. Pioneers in organising drainage works were a Doctor Piotay and the Comte de Saint-Saud, and a monument commemorating their achievements can be seen at Echourgnac.

In certain respects the Double is a very different place today from what it was a century or so ago. Its population has been halved since 1890, the contraction beginning somewhat later than in most parts of Périgord because of the improvements to agriculture and health taking place around 1870. Pastures now interrupt the woodland and support herds of healthy looking dairy cattle, Normandy or Friesian (*Pie Noire*) breeds being more common than local ones. Veal is also raised as in the neighbouring Ribéracois. Recreational activities are catered for to an increasing extent, notably in the vicinity of the Etang de la Jemaye, but visitors also patronise and so help to keep alive some of the old craft industries in places such as Saint-Barthélemy and Saint-Vincent-Jalmoutiers. Another link with the past is the fair held twice a year at La Latière, a wild spot

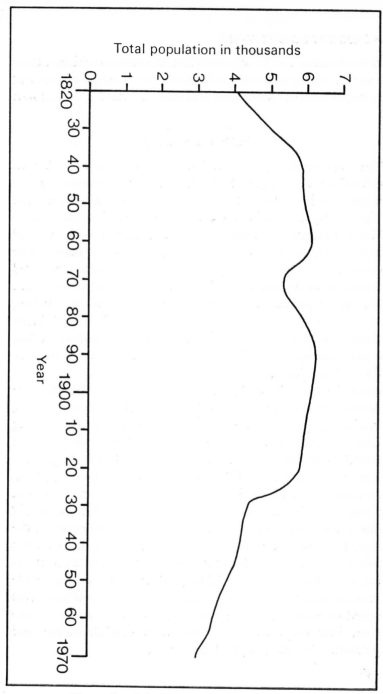

Fig 11   Population trends in the Double, 1820-1970

in the heart of the forest, once the resort of horse thieves. Here and there in the Double one also encounters a simple monument to members of the Resistance who were shot during the last war.

## PAYS DE BELVÈS

The Pays de Belvès is typical of those wooded areas known collectively as Périgord Noir. It is a strip of country, a few kilometres in width, extending south of the Dordogne and bisected by the main road, the N710, running south from Siorac towards the valley of the Lot. To the west, beyond Monpazier, it gives way abruptly to the much more fertile country of the Bergeracois; to the east is an equally contrasted landscape in the limestone Causse of Daglan and Campagnac. The pays takes its name from the small, hilltop town of Belvès, several place-names incorporating the suffix '-de Belvès'. From Belvès itself there are extensive views back towards the valley of the Dordogne, and the town boasts the title of the 'belvédère du Périgord Noir'.

As elsewhere in Périgord Noir, the forests of the Pays de Belvès owe their presence to the blanket of ferruginous sands, in places 15 to 20 metres thick, which covers the underlying Cretaceous limestones. For the most part this layer of superficial deposits consists of reddish-brown sands and gravels, but the farmer who tries to cultivate them is likely to encounter blocks of sandstone and hard nodules of concretionary ironstone. Pockets of china clay betray the fact that these rocks were laid down following erosion of the granite highlands further to the east. Here and there the sands have themselves been eroded but it is to reveal a layer of flints derived from ancient weathering of the limestones and yielding soils that are no more fertile than the rest. For the most part the soils are light and acid, well suited to heath and to a forest of oak, chestnut and maritime pine. Few crops do well under such conditions, rye and potatoes being the principal exceptions.

Like the Double, the Pays de Belvès has been both a frontier between more favoured areas adjacent to it and a place of refuge. It lies on the margins of Périgord, Agenais and Quercy and its marchland role was particularly in evidence during the long struggles between French and English in the Hundred Years War when rival bastides were founded on either side of it. For others it afforded a retreat for contemplation. The great Cistercian abbey of Cadouin was founded early in the twelfth century in a portion of the Pays de Belvès known as the Forêt de la Bessède, and the difficulty and slowness of communications ensured that for several centuries it remained virtually independent of the ecclesiastical authority exercised from Périgueux or Sarlat. The site was more accessible though to travellers following the valley of the Dordogne and the abbey became a place of pilgrimage after it acquired what was believed to be a fragment of the Holy Shroud. A more sceptical age has revealed this to be linen woven in the eleventh century, but in the Middle Ages it attracted many pilgrims and the wealth they brought to the abbey enabled the monks to build what is Cadouin's principal glory, its cloister. Begun at the end of the fifteenth century it is an impressive example of late Gothic decorated architecture, and contrasts sharply with the heavy and more sober twelfth-century church.

Cultivation in the Pays de Belvès, as in the Double, has been confined to clearings in the forest, and the life of a typical peasant family of the last century is graphically described in *Jacquou le Croquant*. Jacquou grew up in the Forêt Barade, but the description applies equally well to any part of Périgord Noir. Pigs were fed on acorns and chestnuts and a few small, coarse-woolled sheep were reared. A little money was earned from the sale of firewood and charcoal and from the mushrooms and cattle litter gathered in the woods. Tannin was obtained from oak bark, and also resin after the maritime pine was permitted to spread in the late nineteenth century. Most of these forest products were sold at markets

147

and fairs held at Villefranche Belvès and Monpazier. The presence of iron-bearing sands gave rise to an iron-making industry like that of the Nontronnais, though on a far smaller scale, and farmers were able to earn a little extra money by digging ore from their fields in shallow pits. Abundant charcoal meant that the ore could be smelted on the spot before it was taken to the stream-side forges where it was made into domestic and farm implements. The forge at La Brame, in the valley of the Dropt near Monpazier, was noted for its ploughshares and was able to employ thirty men in the early years of the nineteenth century. The industry has long since died out in the Dordogne but there is an interesting survival a few kilometres to the south of Périgord at Fumel, in the valley of the Lot. The Grand Central railway company built a couple of coke-fired blast furnaces here in 1847 and under the name of the Société Métallurgique du Périgord the company specialised in equipment for the railways for which the peculiarly shock-resistant qualities of the local ore were well suited. Iron-making has lasted to the present day but is now dependent upon imported ore.

### WILDLIFE

Forty-six thousand permits to shoot were issued in the Dordogne in 1972, a total exceeded in only three other départements of France. As the figure suggests, Périgord is something of a huntsman's paradise and a visit to the local mairie is always remarkable for the array of rules and regulations governing the shooting of what seems to be an infinite number of animals and birds. One has the impression that there would be few left if it were not for these controls and the vigilance of the 350 Sociétés de Chasse that operate in the département. There is also, at departmental level, a federation that concerns itself with game protection and with restocking. It was responsible a few years ago for the reintroduction of the red deer to the Dordogne.

The woods, lakes and rocky caves of the Dordogne constitute an ideal environment for many small animals and birds, whilst the rivers are rich in fish. The region also lies across the migratory path of many species of birds which adds to the variety of wildlife present. Nevertheless there are problems and in Périgord, as elsewhere, the survival of wildlife is increasingly threatened by the use of fertilisers and pesticides, by the proliferation of motor vehicles, and by the grubbing of hedges in connection with remembrement. It is possible to point to the extensive tracts of forest and scrub that are relatively untouched by these manifestations of 'progress' and where wildlife would seem to be secure, but experience has shown that even in these parts protection and control are necessary if the range of fauna is to be maintained.

Wild boar still roam the forests of Périgord as they have for centuries, constituting the most distinctive element in the region's fauna. They are very much a part of the natural ecology of these chestnut and oak woods, but for a long time their numbers declined because of the damage they caused to crops and, occasionally, to humans. Recently they have increased again. One reason for this is the protection they get from limiting the hunting season to just two months, September and October; another is the change in attitude of the farmers brought about by the payment of generous compensation where crop destruction has taken place. There is also a demand for wild boar pâté, and at Montemart between Périgueux and Le Bugue there is a domaine which raises boars under conditions approximating to the wild.

Numbers of roe deer have increased too, and they are a common sight. They have been seen on the streets of Périgueux and, unhappily, several dozen are killed each year on the roads of the département. Some accidents are reported; in other instances it is suspected that the deer is bundled rapidly into the back of the car which drives off. A new name has been coined for this kind of motorist—*automobiliste viandard*. There is a season

when the roe deer can be hunted legally but it may be limited
to as short a period as two days. The recently introduced red
deer is even more carefully protected to the extent that there
may be a controlled shoot of no more than about a dozen head.
They are limited in their distribution to just three localities:
the Forêt de Vieillecour in the high ground of the Nontronnais,
the Double, and the wooded hills south of Domme. Their
numbers have grown least well in the Double, whether this is
from failure to adjust to the natural environment or from
poaching is not fully known.

Rabbits are seen everywhere in the Dordogne having recovered from the effects of myxamatosis, but they are most
common amongst the well-fissured rocks of the limestone areas.
The hare, by contrast, is comparatively rare.

The most popular game bird is the pheasant and large
numbers are shot in the season including both wild birds and
ones which have been reared in captivity. Migratory species
include woodcock and wood-pigeon and also many breeds of
duck which congregate on the region's lakes and rivers during
the winter. Information about hunting and shooting can be
obtained from the *Fédération Départmentale des Chasseurs de la
Dordogne* at 4, Rue Arago in Périgueux. Licences to fish can
likewise be obtained from the *Fédération Départmentale des
Associations de Pêche et de Pisciculture* at 31, Rue du Président-
Wilson in Périgueux, or from the local office of one of the sixty-
eight associations which make up the Fédération.

Périgord boasts 8,000 kilometres of river bank, and with some
hundreds of small lakes, the region is as much a paradise for the
fisherman as it is for the huntsman. The trout is king and has a
fishing season that lasts from the first Saturday in March to the
final Monday in September. But there are numerous fresh-
water species to be caught including eels, roach, tench, carp,
bream, perch and, not least, pike. Fishing from the rivers is
strictly controlled and the casual fisherman with little experience would be well advised to visit one of the many lakes where

there are no restrictions on the length of the fishing season. These are most numerous in the Nontronnais, where the Etang de Saint-Estèphe is a popular resort, the Double and the Landais.

## A TRADITIONAL INDUSTRY: PAPERMAKING

A dozen papermills still operate in Périgord, employing between them some 1,500 workpeople—a valuable contribution to employment in a region where there is little manufacturing industry. Except for water, however, local raw materials no longer contribute a great deal to the industry, and it is inherited skill and specialisation in certain products that has allowed papermaking to survive to the present day.

The importance of skill and tradition is well seen in the three small mills which cluster in the valley of the river Couze just above its confluence with the Dordogne. They are family firms, each employing no more than forty workers of whom a high proportion are female, and they concentrate on the production of very fine papers that are used as filtering agents, mainly by the pharmaceutical and food industries. It is work that involves a large amount of hand labour in, for example, stretching, folding and packing the papers. The mill at Creysse in the Dordogne valley near Bergerac is very similar, with products that include blotting paper and papers for adhesive strips. As raw material the mills use mainly cotton rags, but a quantity of cotton linters is also imported.

Another old-established papermaking district is the one near Thiviers at Nanthiat, Nantheuil and Corgnac in the valley of the river Isle (page 80). There is a small group of mills here, too, which now specialise in the manufacture of finest quality writing papers. Raw materials are principally woodpulp imported from Scandinavia and North America, beechwood pulp from the Pyrenees, and china clay, used for coating the paper, from Cornwall. They can be brought to Thiviers by

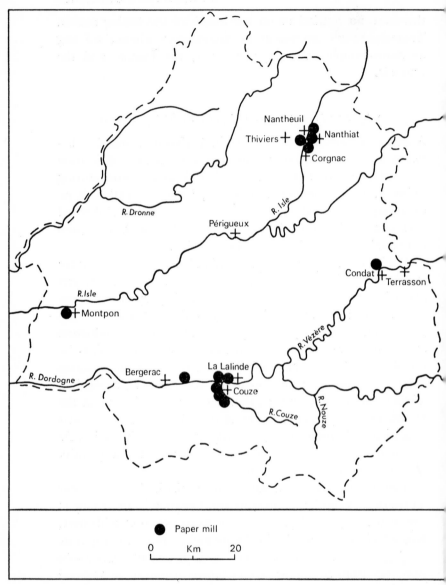

Fig 12   The paper industry in Périgord (after Michel Genty, *Rev Géog des Pyrénées et du S-O*, 1970)

rail, but the cost of assembling materials is high, and survival of the industry in this rather remote valley depends on the reputation which the mills have built up for their products. Some publicity has been obtained recently by printing luxury editions of Georges Rocal's *Croquants du Périgord* and *La Science du Gueule* on paper specially made by the Papeteries de Guyenne.

Further down the Isle valley at Montpon there is an isolated mill that makes paper coverings for a cardboard-manufacturing firm at Seurin. Unlike those at Couze and Thiviers, the site is not very old, papermaking here dating from 1875 when a mill was set up to use local straw and waste paper. It still relies on waste paper collected in Bordeaux.

The paper industry at Condat near Terrasson and at Port-de-Couze in the Dordogne valley has been far more closely related to the forest resources of Périgord than has been the case with the small mills described above. For the latter, the quality of the local water supply, coupled with the availability of power sites, can be said to have been the raison d'être, whereas the mills at Condat and Couze were set up to extract tannin from locally obtained chestnut wood. This they continued to do until as recently as 1956 at Couze and 1960 at Condat, but long before that time the manufacture of cellulose, at first a by-product of the extraction of tannin, had become the main concern of the factories.

The mill at Condat is easily the largest in Périgord, employing some 850 workers, mostly men, who travel daily to the factory from villages and small towns within a radius of about 25 kilometres. Papermaking began in 1930 and Condat is the only mill in the region which remains integrated, producing paper from its own pulp. Some of the lumber used is from nearby forests, but beechwood is also brought in from Limousin and the Auvergne, and the hardwood timbers are supplemented with imported coniferous woodpulp. The Condat factory manufactures paper in bulk for bags and envelopes as well as more exotic papers like the gummed backing on which postage stamps are printed. In 1969 a collector's edition of Eugène Le Roy's novel, *Le Moulin du Frau*, was printed on paper made at Condat. Quantities are also exported.

The Port-de-Couze mill is much smaller than the one at Condat and now specialises in paper which is used for making yoghourt cartons. But there is, in addition, an offshoot of the original tannin-extraction industry at neighbouring Lalinde where 400 are employed in the manufacture of plastic-laminated wood of the kind used for kitchen furniture. Pine and chestnut are the principal raw materials. There is one other papermill in the Couze-Lalinde portion of the Dordogne valley, that of Rottersac. In the nineteenth century the site was a glassworks, and papermaking began only at the beginning of the present century. The firm which at present occupies the mill specialises in high-quality papers for packaging, made from imported woodpulp.

Doubts have been expressed over the future of several of the papermills. They face high costs of assembling materials and of despatching finished products, and their survival seems to depend on a reputation for products which may well face competition from cheaper substitutes in the future. Yet closure could bring severe employment problems to at least three localities—those of Lalinde, Terrasson and Thiviers—where a significant proportion of the population is dependent on the papermills for work. There are thus strong social pressures to keep the mills open. In the longer term it would seem sensible to relate the forest economy more closely to the needs of the industry as has been the case in the Landes, and experiments are already taking place aimed at making better use of the region's chestnut woods.

Page 155 (*above*) Castle of Beynac in the Dordogne valley; (*below*) Renaissance architecture: the castle of Puyguilhem

*Page 156*   Monbazillac: view over the vineyards to the Dordogne valley and the
factories of the Poudrerie Nationale

# 8     THE ART OF BUILDING

FEW parts of France can rival the Dordogne in the fascina-
tion and allure of its buildings. There is no architectural
masterpiece comparable with Chartres or Versailles, no
monuments to the past that can rival Arles or Nîmes, but the
number of castles is enormous and there is a wealth of architectural detail to be discovered and enjoyed in its churches, farms
and cottages. The student of architecture will recognise certain
features that may be described as regional, as *périgordine*,
although in actual fact he will admit that there is little that is
unique to the Dordogne and there are also differences to be
observed within the region. Yet niceties of definition can hardly
detract from the satisfaction that comes from viewing some
castle perched high on a valleyside crag or the cluster of
humbler dwellings, built of local materials, weathered and worn
so that they are in perfect harmony with the rest of the landscape.

## THE CHURCHES

The eleventh and twelfth centuries were ones of spiritual
reawakening in which the various monastic orders played a
large part and many churches were built or rebuilt in the new
*romanesque* style. There are about a thousand churches in Périgord and, of these, over half belong wholly or in part to the
period, some having survived almost unchanged over the
centuries, others having been extensively rebuilt or restored
leaving only foundation walls or a few arches as evidence of
their antiquity. Overall the early Middle Ages have left a great

K

legacy of ecclesiastical building, and if the little country churches lack grandeur, they have a rustic charm that well repays a visit. For the most part they were built by local masons, some of these more skilled or more ambitious than others, and they were used for many purposes, serving not only as a place of worship but as a meeting-place for the community and, in wartime, a defence. It is scarcely to be expected that a Périgord Romanesque style would emerge under such circumstances. Nevertheless certain common characteristics are there to be observed.

Most of the Romanesque churches in Périgord have a very simple ground plan, either rectangular or with transepts which take the form of the Latin cross. Very few have side aisles and this is true even of the present and former cathedral churches of Saint-Front and Saint-Etienne in Périgueux. There are some exceptions, notably at Cadouin and Bussière-Badil, but in general the nave is uncomplicated by pillars and side aisles, and a row of single arches is likely to be seen supporting a barrel-vaulted roof. Blind arches, however, are very common. These are arches built against the wall of the church, both inside and outside, and at first glance it is often difficult to see what purpose they serve since the window openings are usually much smaller and quite out of scale with the arches. Undoubtedly they help to strengthen the walls of the church and it is likely that they were also built for decorative purposes, to relieve what would otherwise have been blank surfaces. Such an idea is borne out when one examines a church like that of Saint-Privat-des-Prés near Ribérac, which has a row of blind arches along both the exterior north and south walls and smaller ones, without any kind of window opening, above the porch on the west wall. The arches give character to what would otherwise be a plain stone box. On the inside of the church the blind arches may project sufficiently far from the wall to support a walk or passage, usually just below the level of small window openings. In time of war, guards could patrol the walk and keep an eye on anyone approaching the church. There is an excellent example at Saint-Amand-de-Coly.

The cupola dome is unquestionably the most distinctive feature of the Romanesque churches in Périgord, although its distribution extends well beyond the limits of the region, from Cahors in the south as far as Poitou and even Anjou in the north. It is most common in the north-west, in Périgord Blanc, but there are examples scattered throughout the region, about 200 domes surviving out of what was certainly a larger number at one time. In most instances a single dome sufficed, above the choir or the crossing, but there are a number of churches which have a row of domes above the nave. There are four in line at Trémolat and again in the church at Cherval near Verteillac. The old cathedral church of Saint-Etienne-la-Cité in Périgueux once had four massive domes, but the building suffered extensive damage during the Wars of Religion and only two survive. One of these has been altered in the course of restoration but the other is almost untouched from the eleventh century and displays all the simplicity of line of the period. It is thought that Saint-Etienne, the mother church of the diocese, was the one which inspired builders to add domes to their churches in other parts of the region.

The question inevitably arises as to the origin of the dome as an architectural feature here in the Dordogne region. Some of the domed churches have an almost Byzantine appearance, suggesting that the idea was brought from the east but, once adopted, the dome would be seen to possess certain advantages. It was more resistant to fire than was the earlier wooden roof and, it has been suggested, it was popular because it offered space over the dome which could be used as a safe hiding place.

The method of support was in most cases by pendentives, triangular-shaped portions of vaulting that fill in the spaces between the piers of the arches and, in effect, convert what would otherwise be a square base into a round one which can bear the dome. Usually the domes are about 4 metres in diameter but there are enormous ones with a diameter of 12, even 15, metres. The largest of all was that at Saint-Jean-de-Côle where the church has no nave but only a huge choir with apsidal chapels opening from it. The dome above the choir was badly supported by unequal arches, so that it collapsed in 1787 and again, after rebuilding, in 1860. After that the space was simply boarded over but the church is still worth seeing, for its unusual design and for its setting in the square of what must be one of the most charming little towns in the whole of the region. The church at Montagrier in the Ribéracois has a somewhat similar plan.

In wartime the church was a refuge and the needs of defence are evident in the solid walls and high slit-like window openings of many of the romanesque churches. Seen from the outside some are more like fortresses than churches and this is particularly the case at Trémolat and Paunat, villages close to the confluence of the Vézère with the Dordogne. Both have massive buttressed walls with narrow windows and their almost identical towers resemble castle keeps. Clearly this was a strategic portion of the Dordogne valley that was particularly vulnerable to attack.

But the finest of the fortified churches is that of Saint-Amand-de-Coly. Cathedral-like in its proportions, it dominates the tiny village at its foot and should be seen first across the valley from the minor road that approaches it from Montignac. From that direction, one has the best view of its enormously high bell tower with its remarkable arch rising above the entrance porch. Built by Augustinian canons as their abbey church, it incorporates a whole system of fortifications which also extended to the hillside immediately behind the church. The wooden structures have gone, but it is not difficult to mentally reconstruct the look-out posts and shooting platforms that must have rested on the projecting stone corbels, and from which arrows and other missiles could be discharged at enemies below. Inside, the floor of the church, paved with heavy stone flags, rises towards the altar because of the slope of the ground against the hillside. The nave seems crude and heavy, but the choir and transepts with their symmetrical chapels display fine workmanship, and the crossing is surmounted by a single dome. The scale is everywhere impressive.

Bell towers like the one at Saint-Amand show just how important were considerations of defence. But the tower at Brantôme is of a very different kind, the need for protection here giving way to artistic expression. It rises in five stages, round arches and high-pointed gables making it a study in interlocking shapes. It is unique in Périgord but was probably inspired by work in neighbouring Limousin where the tower at Saint-Léonard near Limoges is very similar. For a long time the tower was neglected, weeds sprouting from its parapets, but it has recently been cleaned and viewed from the old bridge where its reflection can be seen in the waters of the Dronne, it is one of the most memorable sights in the region.

Brantôme aside, the impression given by most of the romanesque buildings in Périgord is of solidity, even austerity, the latter perhaps owing something to monastic influence. Such an impression is heightened by the rarity of stone carving. There are very few sculptured doorways, for example, and although exceptions can be found—as at Bussière-Badil and Besse—in general masons seem to have wasted little time building the porch. Where carving is found it is generally on capitals, and it is on these that the local mason exercised his talents and imagination, usually confining himself to representations of plants or animals but, if he were more ambitious, recreating scenes of biblical or of everyday life. Artistic licence is abundantly displayed. Sometimes the subject is fantastic, comic, even pornographic, and if the sculptures lack finesse they more than make up for this in vigour. Particularly interesting are the ones in the churches at Thiviers, Cénac (near Domme) and in the remote abbey church of Merlande (in the Forêt de Feytaud, west of Périgueux).

No more than passing reference has so far been made to what must surely count as the most extraordinary church in Périgord, the cathedral church of Saint-Front in Périgueux. Seen from the opposite bank of the Isle, its domes and lantern-like towers make up a composition that is not easily forgotten. Most of what one sees, however, is of nineteenth-century date, the twelfth-century church having been almost totally rebuilt by the architect, Abadie, during the latter half of the last century. Abadie was responsible for the Church of the Sacré-Coeur in Paris, and his Saint-Front has the same unreal quality, looking like some enormous wedding cake. Yet its very size compels attention and it is far from lacking in interest. It is in fact two churches. To the west of the domed church is a portion of an older eleventh-century building, destroyed by fire in 1120, which now presents an imposing courtyard entrance. Inside, Abadie's church is light and airy and its unusual shape, in the form of a Greek cross, has been fully exploited by placing an impressive new altar centrally at the crossing.

In this brief description of the churches of Périgord the emphasis has been placed on the Romanesque period since it is that which has left its imprint most obviously upon the region, 'clothing it in a white robe of churches'. But the styles of later ages were not altogether ignored. South of the Dordogne, near Beaumont, there is a church at Saint-Avit-Senieur which on the outside is a typically fortress-like building of Romanesque style, but inside the roof is supported by Gothic arches. These rest on massive columns which it seems were intended to support three cupolas but the latter were never built. It would be interesting to know why the fashion for pointed arches came to be adopted at an early date in this out-of-the-way spot in the Pays de Belvès. Elsewhere cupolas were deliberately taken down to make way for Gothic vaulting. It happened at Brantôme when the abbey church was transformed in the fourteenth century, and at Thiviers where two cupolas were taken down in 1511 and Gothic arches erected on the same supporting pillars.

Similar 'improvements' took place at Saint-Sacerdos in Sarlat to give the church a style more in keeping with its cathedral status, little more than the bell tower being left of the original romanesque building. Other churches were also altered and new ones, like the bastide churches, were built in the Gothic style although their military appearance often makes this difficult to appreciate from the outside. In general, however, the rebuilding movement was limited by the effects of the Anglo-French wars and the loss of population resulting from the Black Death.

The last flourishes of Gothic architecture are represented by the cloister at Cadouin, built at the close of the fifteenth century. Thereafter the Renaissance introduced classical ideas which are more in evidence in castles and town houses than in ecclesiastical buildings. Yet examples are not wholly lacking in church buildings and amongst these it is worth noting the doorway to the church at Rouffignac and the two-tier cloister at Saint-Jean-de-Côle.

### THE CASTLES

Centuries of war, rebellion and family rivalry has left the Dordogne region with a marvellously rich inheritance of castles. There is scarcely a turning in the Dordogne valley that fails to reveal some imposing structure of towers and pinnacles, and if the other valleys have somewhat fewer castles, it is only a matter of relative abundance. There are well over a thousand of them, ranging in size from the huge complex of Biron to the small, fortified manor or *gentilhommière*. Because of damage suffered in wartime or to the substitution of a new style in building, most have been altered or added to over the course of six or seven hundred years, so that dating or classifying them according to certain selected characteristics is an almost impossible task. Yet despite their diversity of form, all seem to be equally a part of the landscape. Jean Secret has observed 'the mysterious harmony that radiates from such monuments as

Beynac, Castelnaud, Salignac, La Roque-Gageac, Berbi-
guières, and a host of castles whose contours unite in perfect
marriage with the curves of the landscape and the silhouettes of
the villages huddling in their shadow' (*Châteaux en Périgord*,
1963).

Military considerations were not always uppermost in the
minds of the castle-builders, but this was certainly so in the
early Middle Ages when watch-towers, archer-holes and
machicolations had a functional rather than a decorative role.
Later they were often added for their aesthetic effect, but there
is no seventeenth-century whimsy about the earliest structures
at Beynac and the now-ruined Castelnaud where the massively
strong keep was the key to a system of fortifications. Both castles
have 'eagle-nest' sites, high on the cliffs above the Dordogne,
and from both there are breathtaking views over the valley
below. One can imagine the intense rivalry when, in the Hundred Years War, one was held by the English, the other by the
French. The English built the round keep at Castelnaud; across
the river at Beynac the huge square keep dates from the
thirteenth century after earlier works had been destroyed by
Simon de Montfort during the Albigensian crusade. Beynac is
in many ways the most remarkable castle in Périgord, the arche-
typal example. It was the seat of one of the four baronies of
Périgord and still belongs to the Beynac-Beaumont family who
have added to it over the centuries. Attractive features inside
are the great state room, the grand staircase and chapel.

Biron, Bourdeilles and Mareuil were the seats of the other
three baronies of Périgord. The castle of Mareuil dates from
the fifteenth century and is guarded by twin gateway towers,
one of which houses an elegant chapel. Biron and Bourdeilles
both retain older structures. Biron, on a hilltop site in the
extreme south of the region, presents an assemblage of towers,
appartments and linking walls that cover the centuries from
the twelfth to the seventeenth, yet the overall effect is one of
harmony. It was held by the Gontaut family, prominent in the

history of France until the Revolution, and its finest architectural monument is the chapel built in the sixteenth century to house the family tombs. There are also other attractive buildings including a picturesque entrance tower and an unusual portico supported by columns.

Bourdeilles is less complicated than Biron. Its site on a cliff top above the Dronne is reminiscent on a smaller scale of Beynac or Castelnaud. Old houses cluster at the foot of the cliff, some of them built into the soft face of the limestone, and there is a picturesque bridge and watermill, though the latter now functions as an antique shop. Bourdeilles is really two castles. The medieval structure is an imposing fortress, enclosed by a strong wall and dominated by a high octagonal keep bristling with machicolations. It was built after the town had been recovered from the English and was clearly intended to resist any further change of possession. Notwithstanding this, Bourdeilles has had a chequered history and the castle now belongs to the Département of Dordogne. Its other portion, the sixteenth-century *château*, stands apart from the older fortified buildings, heightening the contrast between the two halves. The château is a plain building viewed from the outside, but it is richly decorated inside, especially the 'gilded room' in which it was intended to receive Catherine de Médicis (page 72).

The late fifteenth and early sixteenth centuries witnessed a rebuilding movement in Périgord; many castles were reconstructed and much of what one sees and admires in the region's military architecture is a product of this period. The defeat of the English in 1453 was followed by a century of relative peace during which reconstruction was able to take place, and the urge to rebuild was spurred on by the ideas of the Italian Renaissance that were being introduced to France towards the end of the fifteenth century. Narrow corkscrew staircases lodged in towers gave way to elegant open stairs on a square plan. Arrow-hole openings were replaced by wide mullioned windows, often decorated with tracery and flanked by columns, and roof lines were broken by dormer windows often surmounted by decorative shell motifs. Doorways were framed between pillars and ornate pediments, and elaborate sculptural effects were introduced to cornices, balustrades and friezes. If the walls appeared plain, then an ornamental stringcourse would be added. Defensive considerations were frequently abandoned altogether, but some seigneurs were more cautious or had longer memories than others, and Renaissance ideas were incorporated into structures that still had an aggressively military air about them. The result was sometimes comic, even bizarre.

Credit for introducing the new style in building must go to individuals who had travelled in Italy or who employed Italian artists and foremost amongst these in Périgord was Jeanne de Saint-Astier who built her castle of Les Bories at the end of the fifteenth century. Others copied her work, Les Bories acting as a centre for the diffusion of the new ideas. Set in the broad valley of the Isle above Périgueux, the castle does not occupy an obviously defensible position so that various elements of fortification were retained in the new design—towers and moat for example. But the roof line is pure Renaissance, at once more like the châteaux of the Loire than the old medieval forts of Périgord, and the windows, though simple, are also modern. The staircase, too, is unmistakably in the new style. Built a little later than Les Bories, the castle of Bannes near Beaumont-du-Périgord provides an excellent illustration of how old and new, defence and decoration, could be combined in a single building. Renaissance windows are set in a keep-like tower, and elaborately embellished dormers sprout above deeply carved machicolations. The castle was built by the Bishop of Sarlat who first cleared an older one from the site, and the whole composition has an unreal air about it, suggesting the back-cloth to a Christmas pantomime or an illustration in Grimm's fairy tales.

Other castles show the same attempts being made to introduce a greater degree of comfort and style to the building with-

166

out giving up its defensive role altogether. This is well seen at Jumilhac where the castle stands on a rocky spur above the upper valley of the Isle. The core of the building, solidly constructed of pink granite, is of fourteenth-century date except for some later windows, but this is capped by what must be one of the strangest roof lines in the region, made up of no fewer than ten slate-clad towers. These are pierced with small, triangular openings (*outeaux*) and topped with lead figures representing knights.

Monbazillac is one of the best-known castles in Périgord because of its association with the famous vineyards, and it is also one of the most nearly symmetrical, a rare quality in the region's castles. Built in the second quarter of the sixteenth century, its corner towers and moat give it a military air, but the numerous mullioned windows, including an unusual double tier in the high roof, suggest a purely domestic use. From the terrace at the back it commands a panoramic view over the vineyards and the Dordogne valley around Bergerac. In the Isle valley, the castle of Neuvic exhibits a similar softening of the military façade by delicate carving of embrasures and machicolations. The attraction of Neuvic is enhanced by its position overlooking the river; the same is true of the castle of Losse where a constrained façade is mirrored in the waters of the Vézère, framed by trees. On the side away from the river there is a charming gateway fort that looks out on a moat and courtyard.

Of all the castles in Périgord the one that best represents the Renaissance in architecture is Puyguilhem. There is little pretence at keeping out enemies here. The château is set on a terrace built out of the side of a gently sloping valley, a short distance from the little town of Villars north-east of Brantôme. Seen from the south, the main building is framed between two magnificent towers, one round with a high conical roof, the other basically quadrangular but with its angles cut away and crowned with a pyramidal roof. But the glory of Puyguilhem is the fineness of its sculpture. There is delicate balustrading, highly ornamental machicolations, cornices moulded in a shell motif, and dormer windows embellished in every conceivable way. Despite the detail, the overall effect is harmonious and pleasing. The château was completed in 1530 and one almost expects to see the Loire flowing below.

Puyguilhem belongs to what has been called the 'First Renaissance' because the elaborate ornamentation, so much in evidence there, became more restrained as the sixteenth century progressed and a more formal, classical element was introduced. Columns and pediments tended to replace carved pilasters and decorative flower motifs. Dormers were still popular but an elegant shell-hood was preferred to the exotic display of sculpture encountered at Puyguilhem. The change can be seen at Montréal near Mussidan, a hilltop castle that was built on to older foundations. Its windows are framed between columns and sculptured medallions add the only other flourish of decoration to its walls. Lanquais (west of Couze in the Dordogne valley) is similarly restrained and some of its windows with their solid triangular pediments could well belong to eighteenth-century Bath.

The classical movement reached its climax in Périgord with the building of Hautefort, a monumental edifice which succeeded the much older castle associated with the troubadour, Bertrand de Born. Begun in 1644 it was substantially completed forty years later, totally dominating the town below and commanding distant views. Unhappily a large part of the castle was destroyed by fire during one night in August 1968, but portions remain and also many photographs, so that it can still be appreciated for what it was, and it is at present being restored by its owner with the help of the *Service des Monuments Historiques*. The main building, with its severe, classical proportions, was flanked at each end by square pavilions from which wings extended outwards at right angles to join matching round towers. Pavilions and towers were capped with domes surmounted by small lantern towers. One of the wings was pierced by a gateway, framed by columns, and it is this and the round tower that survived the fire. Hautefort was the most imposing castle in Périgord, its restrained lines and its setting in formal gardens reflecting, as faithfully as Beynac or Puyguilhem, the spirit of the age in which it was built.

Overlooking the Vézère at Aubas, the Château de Sauveboeuf is a more modest expression of the classical school of architecture. It was built in the seventeenth century by the Marquis de Sauveboeuf after an earlier castle had been taken down on the orders of Cardinal Richelieu. It has the same elegant proportions as Hautefort, pavilion wings here too extending at right angles from the main building to form a court that once held two fountains.

Périgord has already been described as a country of squires, and when he was prosperous the local seigneur was as likely to rebuild his house as the great baron. The region has many such gentilhommières, country mansions that reflect the architectural tastes of their day. In the seventeenth and eighteenth centuries the fashion was for building a *chartreuse*. This is a building of essentially one storey, although dormer windows were often added in the high-pitched roof and, in the classical tradition, pavilions were built on the ends to create a terrace or court that could be set off with balustrading or some ornament such as a well or fountain. Always elegantly proportioned, the simplicity of the façade was relieved by indenting or projecting the stonework slightly so that the angles would be picked out by shadow. A formal garden with neatly clipped box hedges would often complete the effect. The best examples of this kind of country mansion are to be found in the Bergeracois, where Le Sautet near the bastide town of Molières and Montbrun (at Verdon) are both outstanding. Not far away, at Bardou, one can see an older château that was 'improved' by the addition of wings and the creation of a garden in the new style. North of the Dordogne at Pézuls there is another charming country residence, Pradelles, with a superb 'Georgian' (Louis XV) doorway and dormer windows with delicate scrollwork set in a mansard roof.

Outside the Bergeracois, Périgord is not rich in eighteenth-century building. One of the few exceptions is the Château of Fayolle at Tocane-Saint-Apre in the valley of the Dronne. It is a building of palladian proportions, exhibiting all the logic and order in its design that is lacking in a castle like Puyguilhem. It illustrates particularly well the formal qualities of the classical revival in architecture, and would not be out of place at the hôtel de ville in some large provincial town.

An even more unusual building to encounter in the Dordogne countryside is the château of Rastignac that overlooks the main road from Périgueux to Brive at La Bachellerie. Built to a rectangular plan, its façade is set off by a semi-circular range of Ionic columns and a high balustrade. Begun towards the end of the eighteenth century, it was completed in 1830 and so closely resembles the White House in Washington (1792–1800) that many attempts have been made to discover whether one building was the inspiration of the other. The matter is still disputed and some have looked for a model of both mansions that has now disappeared. Rastignac was partially destroyed in 1944 but was faithfully restored after the war.

Castles are an essential part of the landscape of the Dordogne and most of them can be seen easily from the outside. A list of those which are open to the public is given in Appendix A. Many of them are as beautiful for their setting as they are for their architecture and some, like Fénelon and Montaigne or the shadowy Château de l'Herm, have become places of literary pilgrimage. They also reveal much about the history of the region. To quote Jean Secret once more:

Its [Périgord's] castles are not lonely monuments set apart from the countryside, but rather, are normal parts of its life and landscapes. They are the rich fabric into which has been woven the thread, sometimes golden, sometimes dark, of the province's history—a history in turn, scandalous and heroic, disappointing and thrilling, criminal and mystical . . . to discover Périgord, there is no better way than to see its castles.

### THE HOUSES

Guidebooks rarely devote much attention to farmhouses and cottages yet it is these, not the castles or churches, that most closely reflect the nature of a region's physical and human environment. Almost invariably built of local materials, their style is influenced by the nature of these materials as well as by the needs, economic and social, of the people who live in them. There is no single house-type unique to Périgord, just as there is no definitive style in ecclesiastical or military architecture, but the rural dwellings of this part of France have sufficient that is distinctive about them to warrant at least a brief description.

Seen from a distance, the feature that strikes one first about a village in the Dordogne is its roofscape. Tiles, weathered and stained, present an irregular pattern of warm, reddish-brown and yellow tints that blend perfectly with their surroundings, being as much a product of nature's hand as of man's. Tiles are used throughout the region as a roofing material but in the Sarladais the older houses are covered with thin slabs of stone known as *lauzes*. Laid almost horizontally, these stone slabs are built up in a kind of pyramid above the house that must impose considerable strain on the oak beams supporting them. They were once employed more widely than at present and at Saint-André-d'Alas near Sarlat there are primitive beehive-type dwellings (restored) which illustrate their very early use. They have also been sympathetically employed in the recent restoration of certain historic buildings like the church at Saint-Amand-de-Coly, and here and there a hamlet can be found where the roofing is entirely in stone. Slate as a roofing material is uncommon except on the borders of Limousin, but it is encountered in places in the Sarladais where the railway made it possible for slate to be introduced.

A distinction can be made between northern and southern France with regard both to the shape of the roof and also to the kind of tiles used to cover it, Périgord lying across the boundary between the two. Périgord Blanc and the Double are 'southern' and have Latin-type roofs which are low-pitched—about 30°— and covered with rounded tiles (*tuiles canals* or 'Roman' tiles). Round tiles are encountered elsewhere too, but the most common form of roof in other parts of the region is one with a much steeper pitch—about 50°—which is covered with flat tiles. A combination of both styles can sometimes be seen in the same group of farm buildings. The slope of the 'northern' roof is typically broken. This may take the form of a mansard roof in which the lower part has a steeper pitch than the upper one. In such a case the upper portion may have a covering of round tiles, flat ones being used for the steeper lower part.

Much more commonly, however, the roof has what is known as a *coyau*. In this case a steeply pitched roof takes on a gentler angle towards its base, and the final three or four rows of tiles are likely to be round ones in contrast with the flat tiles that cover the rest of the roof. The purpose is partly decorative, but the gentler pitch at the ends of the roof ensures better protection from rain for the base of the walls of the house. This is necessary because gutters are rarely used on traditional dwellings. Instead the eaves of the roof are made to project beyond the walls, sometimes by as much as half a metre, or even more. The space between roof and walls is often taken up by a cornice and it is not uncommon for the humblest of cottages to possess a handsome cornice with quite an elaborate dog-tooth design.

A steeply pitched roof affords plenty of space which can be used for accommodation or storage and dormer windows (*lucarnes*) to light this space are a regular feature of houses in the Dordogne. Supported directly above the main walls of the house, these windows are always taller than they are wide and have a small, two- or three-sided gabled roof of their own— never a single projecting roof—which mirrors the slope of the roof of the house as a whole. The simple peasant cottage (*maison paysanne* as opposed to *maison de maîtres*) is unlikely to have such elaborate dormer windows, but instead will possess one or more small, triangular-shaped openings in the roof. Known as *outeaux*, these are very characteristic of cottages in the region and they are now often incorporated in new houses for decoration. There are several ways of building them. When the roof is of stone slabs, the opening may consist only of two stones on end with a third one capping them. More commonly, in a tiled roof, the point of the triangle is made to extend forward from the line of the walls, leaving two sides of the projected opening to be covered with tiles. The purpose of the outeaux was, and to a certain extent still is, to provide ventilation for the loft (*grenier*) where hay or grain was stored.

In contrast with the roof and its dormer openings, the chimney of a house in the Dordogne is rarely an eye-catching feature. Soundly constructed and usually rectangular in section, it is sometimes crowned with a decorative arrangement of tiles but this practice is not very common. Below, the walls of the house are generally built of irregularly shaped blocks of stone bound together with a particularly tenacious mortar made from locally worked clay and lime.

Périgord has been fortunate in having plentiful building materials, including timber and sand, close to hand. Stone need rarely be carried far and is therefore used almost universally as a building material, exceptions occurring only in the Double where old structures have a timber frame with a filling of dried mud, and in parts of the Dordogne valley where large, flat pebbles from the river have been used for walling. The weathered stone imparts its own mellow colours to the buildings, greyish-white in the Bergeracois and Périgord Blanc, shades of red or brown in the Sarladais, and an attractive rose colour where granite is used in the Nontronnais. Even when roughcast has been applied to give the walls an additional protection, it seems to weather to the same colour because it has been made from

L

locally produced lime and sand. Dressed stone is not common
except in those localities where a soft and easily worked
material is available or where some ruined château has provided
a convenient quarry.

Windows are small and few in the maison paysanne. Narrow
like the dormer windows, they are usually made up of four, six
or eight small panes and are protected at night by plain wooden
shutters. In larger houses the windows, as well as being somewhat bigger, are rather more sophisticated in design and tiny,
square panes are often used for the glazing.

In a typical farmhouse in the Dordogne, the family's living
accommodation is on the first-floor and the ground-floor of the
dwelling is given over to a wide range of uses. Here wine is
stored and it also houses a range of tools and implements including, probably, the press in which the wine is made. Depending on the number of other buildings available, a portion of it
may be used for stabling animals. The staircase to the rooms
above is likely to be open, or only partially enclosed, and it
frequently leads first to a covered terrace or small gallery
(*balcon-portique*), another of the most characteristic features of
the Périgord house. Supported by wooden rails, occasionally
even by stone columns, it is a shady spot for grand'mère to sit
on a hot summer's day. It is also ideal for drying almost any-
thing, ranging from clothes to tobacco. Decorated with pots of
geraniums and perhaps a climbing vine, it can be very pretty
and adds colour and interest to an otherwise plain façade.

The *pigeonnier* (pigeon-house) is encountered in many parts
of France, but nowhere is it so common or so charming a
feature of the rural dwelling as in Périgord and neighbouring
Quercy. Many of the larger farms possess one, built usually at
one end or corner of the main building. Most of them are
square or rectangular in plan and are topped with a little
pyramid-shaped roof which rises above the general roof line,
adding character to the distant view of almost any village.
Pigeons were once a valuable supplement to the winter food

supply so that, although towers were confined to the wealthier dwellings, practically every cottage has, somewhere near the top of the wall, a stone with two or three little openings through which the pigeons can reach a portion of the loft.

A factual description of house-types does little to convey the 'atmosphere' of a village which depends, not only upon the nature of individual farms and cottages, but on the arrangement of all the buildings including barns, stables and the miscellaneous outhouses used for geese, chickens or even rabbits. In the Nontronnais, and again in the poorer parts of the Double, these various buildings are generally under one single roof, but in the rest of Périgord they are more likely to be seen arranged loosely around a three-sided court or yard, open to the road. In the centre is the well, often protected by its own little well-house, and still used as an economy measure even if the village is supplied with piped water. The *basse-cour* is always alive with poultry and small animals, a place of constant coming and going, of chatter and even drama.

# 9        TOWN LIFE

PÉRIGUEUX is a palimpsest; its old stones have been used many times and the visitor soon learns to hide his surprise at finding Roman sculpture built into the wall of a modest nineteenth-century house. Sacked by Barbarians, burnt by Normans, besieged by the English, torn apart in the Wars of Religion, divided during the Fronde and finally occupied by the Germans during World War II, the departmental capital of Périgord mirrors in its fabric and in its plan some two thousand years of the region's history.

In 1800 the small provincial town, recently chosen as chef-lieu of the département of Dordogne, had a population of only 5,700. It was a twin town: in the *Cité* to the west houses clustered round what was left of the church of Saint-Etienne and of the Roman Civitas; on higher ground overlooking the river to the east was the medieval bourg of Saint-Front where some elegant streets of town houses had been built in the Renaissance style of the sixteenth century.

Population increased steadily during the first half of the nineteenth century, mainly as a result of the new-found administrative role, and by 1850 the total was around 13,000. Improved navigation on the Isle during the 1830s was both cause and effect of growth, and in 1837 a canal basin was opened to handle the goods that could now be brought by *péniche* (small barge) from Bordeaux. But of much more lasting significance was the arrival of the railway in 1856 and the

176

opening soon afterwards of works for the repair of locomotives and carriages. At their peak the workshops employed as many as 2,000 men and as a result of the prosperity brought by the railway the population of the town grew rapidly from 14,778 in 1860 to 21,864 in 1872. By this latter date the town had spread well beyond the confines of its walls and new roads had been made within the old town itself.

Growth beyond the walls began in the 1830s when several new public buildings were erected: the Palais de Justice, a theatre (where the Palais des Fêtes now stands) and an abattoir, all of them designed by the architect, Catoire. The 1830s also saw the initiation of Périgueux's first municipal water supply, pipes being laid from the great resurgence known as the *Source de l'Abîme* which had once been tapped by the Romans. New building took place even more rapidly in the 1850s, mostly to the north of the town where the *préfecture* was completed in 1861, and a prison in 1863. The station and railway workshops also drew development towards the north-west where Le Toulon became the principal industrial suburb of the town, as it has remained to the present day. Infilling gradually took place along the Angoulême road between Le Toulon and the old town, especially around the church of Saint-Martin, and there gradually emerged what is now firmly established as the business quarter of Périgueux. The latter is delimited fairly precisely by a quadrilateral of busy roads: Rue Victor Hugo (north), Rue du Président Wilson (south), Boulevard Michel Montaigne (east) and the Rue de Metz/Rue de Vassovie (west). Town walls gave way to roads—Cours Tourny, Cours Fénelon etc—and public gardens, the earliest of which, the Allées de Tourny, was laid out in the eighteenth century.

The narrow streets and alleys around Saint-Front remained almost untouched by change until the middle of the nineteenth century, but in 1857 a plan was drawn up to improve access, work on the restoration of the cathedral itself having begun in 1852. The plan involved a number of new roads, including the

Rue Saint-Front and the Rue Pierre-Magne (later known as the Rue de la Républic) which made a more attractive approach to the Hôtel de Ville. Alongside the river, where flooding had long been a problem, the road that carries a portion of the N21 was constructed over the Rues Neuves and a new *quai* was built along the river frontage between the two bridges, the Pont de Saint-Georges (1767) and the Pont des Barris. Unfortunately the new engineering works could not be carried out without loss to some handsome old buildings. The Rue Saint-Front opened up a vista of the cathedral but destroyed the hôtel de Saint-Aulaire, whilst the riverside works removed several watermills and the ancient bridge, hump-backed, fortified and built on the angle, which was replaced by a straight, modern structure (the present Pont des Barris) in 1873.

After about 1880 the growth of the town slowed down as economic depression affected the region as a whole. There was some migration from the countryside to the towns but apart from the railway workshops, Périgueux had little industry that could provide much employment. A list of the activities carried out at this time would have included the manufacture of nails, woollen cloth, hats, wax candles and earthenware, as well as grainmilling, foundry work, stone polishing and the making of aniseed liqueurs. But they were all small enterprises, catering essentially for local or, at best, regional needs and few were in a position to absorb more workers. By 1911 the town's population had increased to only 33,548, and a general air of stagnation lasted through the interwar years. By 1937 the total population had risen very slightly to 37,615. Bitter political quarrels made it difficult to carry out improvements to the town and little came of a plan published in 1930. A new post office was completed in 1931 and a rather austere looking hospital, but there were few other additions of note.

With the outbreak of World War II the population was suddenly swollen by the arrival of some 25,000 refugees from Alsace, and for a time Périgueux acted as a kind of Strasbourgin-exile. Although the town was in Unoccupied France, the strength of the Resistance later attracted a German garrison that occupied it for twenty-one months before its liberation in August 1944. For a time during the war the population exceeded 60,000, imposing a severe strain on accommodation and services. Most of the refugees later returned to their former homes, but renewed prosperity in the postwar years has resulted in a steady population growth that added some 12,000 to the total between 1946 and 1968.

Périgueux, with its suburbs, again has a population of around 60,000 and this is expected to rise to between 70,000 and 80,000 by 1985. Use of the private motor car has meant that practically all the growth has taken place outside the actual commune of Périgueux in suburbs such as Chamiers, Trélissac and Boulazac. West of the river, at Chamiers, land was available for building on the site of a former racecourse, and extensive development has taken place with blocks of flats as well as individual houses. What amounts virtually to a 'new town' has been created, but there is only limited employment and few services available, so that heavy traffic is forced to converge daily on the one rather tenuous link with Périgueux, the Pont de la Cité.

Across the river to the east, the suburb of Boulazac has grown up around a new industrial estate, reducing the need for commuting, and a large amount of new housing has been erected here in the last few years. Beyond these inner suburbs, a wealthier middle-class population is swelling the numbers in villages such as Chancelade and Champcevinel to the north, Coulounieix and Notre-Dame-de-Sanilhac to the south. Houses are detached, set in their own gardens and many examples can be seen of houses built in 'le vieux style périgordin', with steep roofs, weathered tiles and outeaux. A certain amount of urban renewal has taken place within Périgueux itself, notably around the Avenue d'Aquitaine which has become something of a showplace with its Palais des Fêtes and new shops, but little has yet been done to replace the old houses, some of them fifteenth century in date, that were pulled down several years ago on the steep slope between Saint-Front and the river.

Périgueux is far from being a major centre of manufacturing industry and a high proportion of its employment is, in fact, in the various categories of service occupation. Nevertheless with over 5,000 employed in manufacturing, the town is the largest single centre of industry in the region. Two-thirds of the work-force is male and most of these find work in the engineering or construction industries. In the first of these categories, the rail-way workshops still account for by far the largest proportion of jobs, employing some 1,800 men and supporting directly about one-tenth of the town's total population.

The railway engineering industry dates from 1864 when the Paris-Orléans company transferred some of its activities from Decazeville to Périgueux in order to take advantage of what was thought to be an abundant supply of labour in Périgord. The main workshops were established near the railway station at Le Toulon but later, in 1917, a second plant was opened on the site of an abandoned army camp at Chamiers on the other side of the river. Until 1954 the workshops were concerned with the repair of both locomotives and carriages, but the abandonment of steam has meant the end of work on loco-motives. Great pride used to be taken in this work and the con-version of the workshops in the late 1950s was not carried through without regrets. The works at Le Toulon now employ 1,400 men in the carriage-repair work and at Chamiers there are 400 employed in the manufacture of welded rails, points and related equipment for the permanent way. Apart from railway engineering there is only a small amount of work available in other branches of the metal industry. Most of this is to be found in the manufacture of metal boxes for the canning industry and in the old-established industry of wire-drawing for the making of staples, barbs, etc. Raw materials have to be brought from outside the region; sheet metal from Nantes and rods for wire-making from Lorraine.

The other industries of Périgueux employ a high proportion of women. The variety of trades is an impressive one but most of the firms are small and few of them are expanding their activities. Amongst the more dynamic firms is one making plastic toys, mainly for the Paris market. It employs about 120 in the factory, but a larger number of women than this work part-time in their own homes. The textile industry is a traditional one and there are about ten small factories engaged in the manufacture of slippers, women's shoes and underwear, and ready-made clothing for men. Reorganisation within the French textile industry and competition from other Common Market countries is making it increasingly difficult for small firms of this kind to survive, and there have been one or two closures recently.

Equally traditional is the food industry, and although the future here seems rather more secure, it is by no means a rapidly expanding industry. It is mainly concerned with confits and pâtés, especially those with a goose liver base, but there are also factories for processing and preserving vegetables and mushrooms. Goose liver is obtained from many small farms in Périgord where, for four or five weeks in November and December each year, the geese are force-fed in order to enlarge their livers. Some of the other ingredients, poultry and truffles for example, are in part locally produced, but much has to be brought in from other parts of France or even from abroad. Such imports may well include venison and wild boar from central Europe, hares from the Soviet Union, partridge from Poland, even larks and thrushes which are obtained from Tunisia. There is a steady market for all these exotic preserves in the luxury food trade, but it is unfortunate that the industry is not based more completely on the produce of its own region. Changes currently taking place in agriculture and wildlife conservation may do something to remedy the situation.

The remaining industries of Périgueux are all small scale and few of them employ more than a handful of workers. They include the processing of tobacco, brush- and basket-making, saw milling and the manufacture of sacks and paper bags. Concern over the town's failure to attract new manufacturing employment was the motive behind the creation of the industrial estate at Boulazac close to the main road and railway to Brive. Choice of this site was opposed by some who felt that the estate should have been established downstream of the town in order to reduce problems of transport, of commuting from the western suburbs, and the discharge of effluent. For a long time the argument remained a largely academic one, no employers of any consequence being attracted from outside the region but recently, however, government pressure aimed at decentralising industry from Paris has led to the establishment of a stamp-printing industry and it is hoped that in time this will become a large employer of local labour.

### La Cité

Tourism must be included amongst the economic activities of Périgueux, but the visitor must be warned that the town does not give the appearance of catering strongly for tourists, and the number of hotels is surprisingly small. There is none of the obvious concern for visitors that can be seen at Sarlat, Les Eyzies or Domme, and some of the shops still close for a period in August. A visit to the Roman Cité leaves a strong impression that other towns would have done more to exploit their ruins. However, if the first reaction is of disappointment it should not discourage further investigation, because the charm of the Cité lies less in its set pieces than in the fragments of wall or sculpture that the visitor is likely to discover in the least expected places.

A visit to the Cité might well begin at the site of the *arena* where the shape and extent of the public garden is the only real clue to the size of what must once have rivalled the arenas of

182

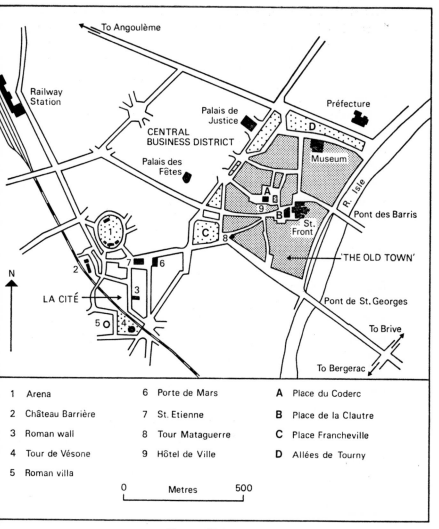

To Angoulème

Railway Station

Palais de Justice

Préfecture

CENTRAL BUSINESS DISTRICT

Palais des Fêtes

D

Museum

A

9

B

St. Front

C

8

R. Isle

Pont des Barris

'THE OLD TOWN'

N

1

7

6

2

LA CITÉ

3

Pont de St. Georges

5

4

To Brive

To Bergerac

| 1 | Arena | 6 | Porte de Mars | **A** | Place du Coderc |
| 2 | Château Barrière | 7 | St. Etienne | **B** | Place de la Clautre |
| 3 | Roman wall | 8 | Tour Mataguerre | **C** | Place Francheville |
| 4 | Tour de Vésone | 9 | Hôtel de Ville | **D** | Allées de Tourny |
| 5 | Roman villa | | | | |

0     Metres     500

**Fig 13    Périgueux**

Nîmes or Arles. Considerable imagination is needed to create a mental picture of gladiatorial combat from the few steps and arches that remain. Destruction of the arena was begun by Barbarian invaders in the third century; later the Count of Périgord built a castle in the ruins, but it was attacked and destroyed in the late fourteenth century by the citizens of Saint-Front, who subsequently used the whole site as a quarry for building stone.

Crossing the busy Rue Chanzy brings one to an excavation where a portion of the third-century Roman wall can be seen and the remains of one of its four gates, the *Porte Normande*, so called because of the part it played in the defence of the Cité against Viking invaders. Nearby, in a small garden, stands what is without doubt the most intriguing collection of buildings in the Cité. The *Château Barrière* is a medieval fortified house with a fine doorway and other additions in the style of the Renaissance, the whole no more than a shell since it was burnt during the Wars of Religion. At one corner stands a strongly built, twelfth-century tower and, at the other, a wall with remains of a bastion leads to what is known as the *Maison Romane*; built over a vaulted crypt, the latter represents the remains of another fortified house, the Château d'Angoulême. But interest lies principally in the foundations and lower walls of these medieval buildings in which massive blocks of stone have been used from older Roman structures. Fragments of columns and capitals can be seen, with stones hollowed out for holding water, and under the bastion a ditch full of sculptured blocks that seem to await sorting like some antique jigsaw puzzle.

A short walk along the Rue Turenne brings one to the Rue Romaine where another section of city wall is to be seen and, at the end of it, the *Tour de Vésone*. Beyond that are the foundations of a Roman villa that has been excavated. The Tour de Vésone is the most imposing monument to Roman Périgueux, a massive tower in stone and brick, some 27 metres in height and 20 metres in diameter, that once formed the core of a temple. Only a few pieces remain of the range of columns that once made a colonnade, or *peristyle*, around the tower. It was the focal point of the Roman city, standing in the market place, and from it roads converged from other parts of the Roman province. There is still a busy road junction at this point but the tower is detached from it and almost undermined by the railway cutting that scores an unsympathetic gash through the heart of Roman Vésone.

From the railway bridge the Rue Emile-Lafon leads to the *Porte de Mars*, another of the city gates but not easy to see because of later building and, nearby, the much-battered *Saint-Etienne de la Cité*. The church was built, symbolically, on the site of a Roman temple dedicated to Mars, and until 1669 it served as cathedral church of the diocese despite the destruction it suffered at the hands of the Protestants in 1577. Reference was made in Chapter 8 to the architectural significance of Saint-Etienne which, despite its misfortunes, is still an impressive structure. A visit might include a glance at the *Chapelle Saint-Jean* (across the road in the convent of Sainte-Marthe) which has a fine Gothic vaulted ceiling with sculptured medallions. It is the only remaining portion of the bishop's palace, also destroyed in 1577.

### Saint-Front—the old town

A walk through the Cité leaves one with no impression that this was once a complete town; the Roman monuments are scattered amongst a mass of later building. The opposite is true of the medieval bourg that grew up around the church dedicated to Saint-Front, and despite the intrusion of new roads in the nineteenth century, it is still recognisably 'la vieille ville'. It is best approached from the direction of the Cité across the Place Francheville which was deliberately left free of buildings, acting as a no-man's-land between the rival settlements. Ahead is the *Tour Mataguerre*, the only surviving part of the fortifications which once included no fewer than twenty-eight such towers. From the top a fine view can be obtained over the old and new parts of Périgueux.

The old town is threaded by so many narrow streets that an itinerary is difficult to plan, and to follow one is to risk missing some of the many delightful old houses that are tucked away in obscure alleys and courts. Old Périgueux is less obviously a Renaissance town than is Sarlat, but it has a wealth of buildings that date from the fifteenth, sixteenth and seventeenth centuries which are best discovered by simply wandering through the streets, referring to the guidebook only when some particularly arresting house invites further study.

If time is short, a good impression can be gained from the streets that lie just to the north of the Place de Coderc: the Rues de la Sagesse, Eguillerie, Limogeanne and the Rue de la Miséricorde. Here are ornate façades like that of the *Maison du Pâtissier* (Rue Eguillerie) and the *Maison Estignard* (Rue Limogeanne), intricately sculptured doorways (see no 11 Rue de la Sagesse and nos 3 and 12 Rue Limogeanne), and elegant staircases (no 1 Rue de la Sagesse and no 2 Rue de la Miséricorde). Other distinguished houses can be seen in the Rue du Plantier, but this lane is remarkable for its traditional form of paving using pebbles from the river with stone slabs for the gutters and for the pathway that runs down the centre of the street. No concession to the motor car here. The Rue Port-de-Graule is similar, though less elaborate. It featured in the film made a few years ago about the life of Jacquou le Croquant. Any visit to Périgueux should include a view of the old town from the river and the best one is from the Pont des Barris, taking in not only the domes and lanterns of Saint-Front but also buildings bordering the river—to the left of the bridge a half-timbered structure that once served as a granary; to the right a picturesque group of fifteenth- and sixteenth-century houses with decorative galleries and lavishly sculptured dormer windows.

Here and there in the old town the narrow lanes are interrupted by small *places*, scenes always of animation especially on market days. The Hôtel de Ville, once the house of the satirical writer Lagronge-Chancel, looks out on a small square which occupies the site of a former church. On its northern side is the Hôtel Gilles-Lagrange, a good example of a fortified town house, built as late as the seventeenth century during the troubles of the Fronde. The *halle* stands on the site of the Consulat, medieval equivalent of the town hall, and overlooks another little square, the Place Coderc, which has survived as an open space because for centuries it provided common grazing for the citizens' pigs. It also held the town well, no doubt a source of many diseases. The square was paved during the sixteenth century and on market day in the winter months, fat geese, foie gras and truffles are sold both here and in the adjoining Rue des Chaînes.

Another lively market is held in the Place de la Clautre which is overlooked by the cathedral. There stood the gallows, and market stalls are now erected on what served in the Middle Ages as the town burial ground. The cathedral itself is an arresting site and although it is fashionable to mock the work of the restorer, Abadie, it is a building that repays a visit. Inside it is possible to forget the fussy lanterns which crown the domes and one can admire the skill of the masons who constructed this vast, airy interior. Outside, it is possible to walk over the roof, amongst the domes, and admire the view of the town, the river and the wooded countryside beyond.

## BERGERAC

Bergerac has grown up on the north bank of the Dordogne where a sloping river terrace gave the town protection from the occasional severe flood. It is likely that at most times the river could be forded at this point and a number of small tributary valleys, like that of the Coudeau, which converge on the Dordogne, ensured that several routeways used the river crossing. The earliest bridge was completed about the year 1209 and a succession of them have followed on more or less the same site, older ones usually having been destroyed by flooding. The river, itself, was navigable for small craft and attempts were made from time to time to improve it. At Bergerac goods would be transferred from water to land and vice versa and *quais* were built downstream of the bridge. The present port dates from the 1820s. As well as acting as an entrepot, the town also served as a market for its own rich and varied agricultural hinterland. The valley of the Dordogne widens out at Bergerac and a broad alluvial plain is backed by river terraces which give way, in turn, to the rolling hills of the Landais to the north and the well-dissected country around Monbazillac to the south—the Bergeracois.

Growth of the town began on the site of a Gallo-Roman villa but there was probably very little in the way of urban settlement until a church was founded by the monks of a nearby priory sometime in the eleventh century. Dedicated to Saint-Jacques, it served as a place of worship for pilgrims following the valley of the Dordogne on their way to Compostela. The bridge attracted trade but it also made the town vulnerable to attack, and in 1345 it was captured by the English who subsequently held it for long periods. The English were finally expelled from the district in 1450. Prosperity followed; a new bridge was completed in 1513 and a large number of hostelries bore witness to the growth of commerce.

During the sixteenth century Bergerac became a stronghold of reform and has been described as the 'Geneva of France'. Henry of Navarre was a frequent visitor to the town which benefited from Protestant emphasis on the virtues of hard work and education. A press was set up to print theological works and a college was founded. The end of the sixteenth century marked Bergerac's 'golden age' and new houses were built like the *Maison Peyrarède* where Louis XIII stayed on his

*Page 189* Typical farmhouse in the Dordogne: both flat and rounded tiles are used, and the characteristically shaped roof is broken by small, triangular openings known as *outeaux*

*Page 190* Aerial view of Périgueux: Saint-Front and the outline of the 'old town' are clearly visible

visit to the town in 1621. It is said that on this occasion fountains flowed with wine, both white and red.

It is interesting to speculate upon what might have happened
to Bergerac if its fortunes had continued, but this was not to
happen. There were indications of what was to follow when
Richelieu ordered the town walls to be taken down. They were
later rebuilt, but destroyed once again during the Fronde.
Various pressures began to be imposed upon the Protestant
community until, finally, in 1685 the Revocation of the Edict
of Nantes was followed by widespread persecution. Large
numbers left the town, many of them to emigrate through the
port of Bordeaux, and within a relatively few years the population of Bergerac had been halved. Outbreaks of plague and the
particularly severe winter of 1709 which destroyed many of the
vines and walnuts, made the situation worse. There was little
trade and as a result the eighteenth century was, by comparison
with the previous one, a century of stagnation and depression.
The majority of the population retained their Protestant sym-
pathies and thus the town continued to be looked upon with
disfavour by the authorities. After the Revolution it became a
*sous-préfecture* of the new département, the administrative centre
of one of the five (now four) arrondissements into which Dordogne was divided.

Bergerac has never lost its liberal, Protestant tradition. It
was, for example, the last town in the département to accept the
accession of Louis-Napoleon in 1848. During the present century its economy has recovered and in the postwar period it has
profited considerably from the changes that have taken place in
the agriculture of the lower Dordogne valley. Between 1962 and
1968 the population increased by 8 per cent and has now reached
30,000.

There are a number of light industries in the town, their
products including agricultural machinery, sandals, and saddle-
bags for cycles and motorcycles. The largest enterprise is the
Poudrerie Nationale (employs 500) situated a few kilometres to

the east of the town in the Dordogne valley, which in peacetime concentrates on the manufacture of nitro-cellulose, used as a base in the production of paints, varnish and various plastics. There are a few small works making these light chemical products in Bergerac itself. The main concern of the town is, however, with the agriculture of its surrounding area. There are corn mills, distilleries and factories making milk products and cattle feed, but the reputation of Bergerac is principally based on three items: wine, preserves and tobacco.

The slopes of the lower Dordogne valley yield the only commercial quantities of high-quality wine produced in Périgord: some 300,000 hectolitres a year, 60,000 of which is Monbazillac. Until the sixteenth century most of the wine came from the sunny south-facing slopes above the east bank of the river, but under monastic influence the hills around Monbazillac began to be planted during that century and it is these vineyards that have subsequently enjoyed the highest reputation. The southern bank is said to possess two advantages which contribute to the quality of the wine: its clay soils (those to the north are gravelly) and its tendency to morning fogs in early autumn. The latter encourage the 'noble rot', the skin of the grapes becoming permeable so that evaporation takes place and the bunches look prematurely dry. This gives the wine its distinctive bouquet and it also has a high alcohol content, averaging 15° to 16°.

Wine is bottled both on the *propriété* and at a number of co-operatives scattered through the wine-growing district, but Bergerac acts as commercial focus of the trade with organisations such as the Conseil Interprofessionnel des Vins. The town is also a centre of the conserves industry, although in this it is rivalled by the smaller settlement of Eymet, a bastide in the valley of the Dropt to the south. The first factory was established at Bergerac in 1882 and for many years the emphasis was on the traditional Périgord products of foie gras and confits of poultry and meat, but the spread of irrigated fruit and

192

vegetable cultivation has widened the scope of the industry to include jam manufacture, fruit-bottling and the preserving of peas, beans, tomatoes, asparagus and gherkins.

Bergerac occupies a unique position in the French tobacco industry, a consequence of the importance of the Dordogne valley for tobacco cultivation. Nearby is the only experimental institute in the country for research into the use of tobacco, and in a part of the Hôtel de Ville there is a museum devoted to the history of tobacco, again the only one of its kind in France. Four sections of the museum are given over to the history of the plant, its cultivation and preparation, the pipes in which it is smoked, and the world trade in tobacco.

With the exception of the tobacco museum and the cathedral —built by Abadie in the 1850s—the attention of the visitor is likely to be confined to the old town, the narrow, confused streets of which are in sharp contrast with the far more spacious and well-ordered modern town that surrounds it. The old town, roughly rectangular in shape, is clearly bordered on three sides by the Rue Saint-Esprit, the Rue de la Résistance, the Rue Neuve-d'Argenson and, on the fourth, by the river. Protective ditches once flanked the old town where the three roads now run. They were supplied with water from the river Coudeau which was dammed for the purpose, and in time of peace they acted as fish ponds, keeping fresh the salmon or carp that were reserved for privileged visitors to the town. Roads were made after the ditches had been filled with stone from the walls pulled down on the orders of Cardinal Richelieu. Foundations of the wall can still be seen, however, in the cellars of buildings along the south side of the Rue de la Résistance— formerly the Rue du Marché and now the principal shopping street in Bergerac.

A good way of seeing the old town is to follow the *Grand' Rue*, or Rue Royale, which used to be the main thoroughfare winding its way through the town from a bridge which lay just downstream of the present one. The street now known as the

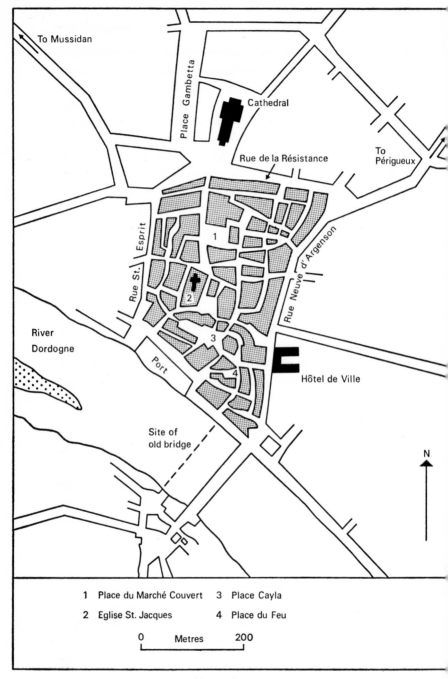

To Mussidan

Place Gambetta

Cathedral

Rue de la Résistance

To Périgueux

Rue St. Esprit

Rue Neuve d'Argenson

River Dordogne

1

2

3

4

Port

Hôtel de Ville

Site of old bridge

N

1  Place du Marché Couvert    3  Place Cayla

2  Eglise St. Jacques          4  Place du Feu

0        Metres        200

Fig 14    Bergerac

Rue de l'Ancien Pont was, in fact, a part of the Grand' Rue and the way by which travellers entered the town from the south; it continues northwards by what is now the Rue des Fontaines. To the modern visitor who comes by car, however, the best approach is from the north since there are car parking facilities in the Place Gambetta. Entry to the Grand' Rue is directly opposite the cathedral and it leads first to the Place du Marché Couvert. The square is interesting for its associations, for here stood the great Protestant meeting-house or temple, destroyed totally in 1682. A gable and angle-tower are the remains of a fortified house in which Catherine de Médicis and her young son, Charles IX, stayed on a visit to Bergerac in 1565.

Continuing southwards, the *Church of Saint-Jacques* reveals little of its long history. Like so many other buildings in Bergerac, and especially churches, it suffered in the Wars of Religion, being rebuilt in the seventeenth century and restored again in the 1860s. The Rue Saint-James and the Rue des Fontaines have some attractive old houses of fourteenth- (*la Vieille Auberge*) and fifteenth-century date and more can be seen if a short detour is taken along the Rue des Conférences and the Rue de la Mirpe.

The Rue des Fontaines leads to the Place Cayla and the chapel and cloister of a Franciscan convent. The former now serves as the Protestant church, and the rest of the building houses the headquarters of the Conseil des Vins. The Rue d'Albret takes one to the Place du Feu, so called because of a fire which destroyed property there in 1820, and the Rue de l'Ancien Pont. There are more interesting houses here of which the most complete is the *Maison Peyrarède*, typical of the houses built by wealthy merchants in the 'golden age' of Henry IV's reign. Having reached the river it is worth following the quais for a view of the port and the warehouses that were built in the eighteenth century for storing grain before shipment. On the site of the quais once stood the castle of Bergerac, dismantled at the same time as the town walls in the 1620s.

### SARLAT

Sarlat is a romantic painting, an engraving, a harmony of
buildings, inviting the poet, the photographer and the painter.
René Deguiral

During the first week in August each year, a festival is held in
the Place Royale in the centre of Sarlat. Plays and concerts are
presented on a specially constructed stage and banks of seats are
erected. But no scenery is required; floodlit, the Church of
Sainte-Marie and hôtels (ie large, imposing houses) of the
fifteenth, sixteenth and seventeenth centuries, provide an in-
comparable back-cloth. Furthermore, if space for staging the
plays were available, a similar setting could be found in almost
any other part of Sarlat, for the town preserves the most remarkable collection of Renaissance buildings in Périgord and
has few rivals anywhere in France.

Yet despite its obvious appeal to the tourist, Sarlat must not
be dismissed as an architectural museum. It still serves as
market town for the surrounding area of Périgord Noir and
every Saturday the narrow streets are thronged with stalls and
bustle. Several fairs are held in the course of the year, and the
trade in walnuts is still an active one. The *énoisement* is a
traditional time for visiting and merry-making in one another's
houses. Foie gras and confits are made and there are a number
of light industries—tanning, ceramics and the manufacture of
electronic and telephone equipment—which help to check the
drift of young men away from the town. Sarlat has a total
population of some 9,000, having recorded an increase of nearly
10 per cent between 1962 and 1968. Most of this increase, it
must be admitted, was at the expense of the rural Sarladais.
Like Bergerac, the town has the status of sous-préfecture.

Situated several kilometres north of the Dordogne in a con-
stricted portion of the valley of the little river Couze, there is no

obvious reason why a town should have grown up on the site of Sarlat. Within the old town, houses cling to the steep valley sides and tortuous lanes are an indication of the cramped nature of the topography. Encircling boulevards were made when the town walls were taken down in 1750, but it is only in the last year or two that any further attempt at a bypass has been made and when in the nineteenth century a new road was required, it was cut in a straight line through the middle of the town. This road, the Rue de la République but known locally as *La Traverse*, was made in the late 1830s and, in a modern, preservation-conscious age, must be regarded as an extraordinary act of vandalism. The wound has healed somewhat with the passage of time, however, and the Traverse has, at least, given Sarlat a convenient shopping street, attractive if it were not for the traffic that often chokes it. Restrictions of site have compelled more recent extensions of the town to spread in a linear fashion along the valley to north and south, continuing the line of the Traverse.

A Benedictine abbey, founded sometime between AD 820 and 840 provided the nucleus around which Sarlat grew, and without such a catalyst it is unlikely that a town would ever have emerged in this rather unpromising spot. A small courtyard immediately south of the present cathedral is the site of the original abbey. Remoteness was an advantage to the new foundation which thereby avoided the pillaging raids of the Vikings, and monks from elsewhere took refuge at Sarlat, bringing their treasures for safekeeping. In this way the abbey acquired the relics of the saint, Sacerdos. By the twelfth century it was sufficiently large and powerful to attract the attention of the Pope who conferred privileges upon it and gave a large number of parishes into its patronage. A new church was built and in 1317 this became the cathedral of a newly formed diocese carved out of the existing diocese of Périgueux, its western and southern boundaries defined by the Vézère and Dordogne rivers. Sarlat retained its bishopric until the Revolution.

Rapid ecclesiastical progress meant that craftsmen, traders and others who wished to serve the abbey were drawn to the town and it is believed that Sarlat had a population of 6,000 in the early fourteenth century. Not all of the latter were sub-servient to the abbey, however, and the subsequent history of the town is marked by a struggle for power between church and townsfolk, the latter represented by their *consuls*. There was little further progress during the protracted Anglo-French wars and the population declined, but after 1450 a period of rebuild-ing began, encouraged by the granting of various royal privi-leges. The next 250 years saw the addition of the hôtels and other buildings for which Sarlat is famous and the town was fortunate in having a large number of citizens wealthy enough to build these three- and four-storeyed houses in the fashionable styles of the time. Bishop and chapter vied with the president and officials of the newly created *Présidial*, each anxious to impress and retain the support of the townspeople. Built of stone and roofed for the most part with lauzes, the houses have resisted decay, and the very slow growth, and at times even contraction, of Sarlat's population has meant that there has been little incentive or pressure to replace them. Only in the present century has the population exceeded the total that was reached in the fourteenth century.

By mid-eighteenth century Sarlat had achieved substantially its present form. The fortifications gave way to *promenades* and the Intendant of Guyenne, Tourny, was responsible as he had been at Périgueux for the creation of a tree-lined garden on the edge of the old town. This, the Grande Riguadie, is still there. It has acquired a statue of Sarlat's best-known literary figure, Etienne de La Boétie, and its shady carparking makes it the best place from which to begin a walk through the streets of the old town.

Opposite the Grande Rigaudie, the Rue Tourny leads to the Place du Peyrou and the cathedral. On the right of the road, the former bishop's palace has a rather austere façade and the in-

198

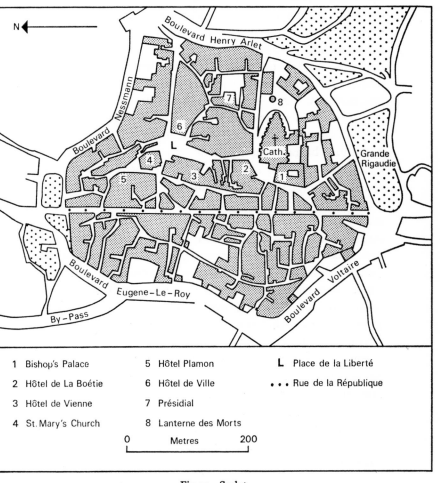

N

Boulevard Henry Arlet

Boulevard Nessmann

Boulevard Eugene-Le-Roy

By-Pass

Boulevard Voltaire

7

8

6

L

Cath.

4

3

2

1

5

Grande Rigaudie

| 1 | Bishop's Palace | 5 | Hôtel Plamon | **L** | Place de la Liberté |
|---|---|---|---|---|---|
| 2 | Hôtel de La Boétie | 6 | Hôtel de Ville | ••• | Rue de la République |
| 3 | Hôtel de Vienne | 7 | Présidial | | |
| 4 | St. Mary's Church | 8 | Lanterne des Morts | | |

0    Metres    200

**Fig 15   Sarlat**

terior, much altered, is now used as a theatre and palais des fêtes. The *Church of Saint-Sacerdos*, still known as the cathedral, was almost wholly rebuilt during the sixteenth and seventeenth centuries after the earlier, Romanesque building had been demolished in 1504, apparently when it was on the point of falling down. Portions of the old church were left, however, most notably the tower which is unmistakably Romanesque despite later additions which include a curiously bulbous steeple, the whim of an eighteenth-century bishop. A visitor to Sarlat in the eighteenth century, Monsieur Latapie, Inspector of Manufactures, described the façade of the cathedral as 'so dreadfully baroque that one doesn't know how to define it'. Facing the entrance to the cathedral, the *Hôtel La Boétie* is, by contrast, one of the most distinguished Renaissance houses in Sarlat. Built in the early sixteenth century, its gabled façade is intricately sculptured, with particularly detailed work around the windows. It was the home of Etienne de La Boétie, friend of Montaigne, who died here in 1563 at the age of thirty-three.

From the Place du Peyrou the Rue de la Liberté with its attractive arcaded shops leads to the Place de la Liberté (or Place Royale). But it is worth taking an alternative route, following a path that leads under an arch of the Boétie house. This threads its way through the courtyards of a collection of fifteenth- to seventeenth-century houses that have only very recently been restored. Before 1970 these courts were inaccessible to the visitor; now it is possible to escape from the traffic and savour a domestic atmosphere that is wholly of the past. The path emerges in the Place de la Liberté where it is overlooked by another showpiece, the sixteenth-century *Hôtel de la Vienne* (or *Hôtel de Maleville*). The doorway is flanked by columns and surmounted by medallions representing Henry IV and his queen; behind it is a particularly fine staircase and the part of the building that houses it has a projecting round tower. A wing to the house terminates in a decorative gable, reminiscent of La Boétie's, and contains an elaborate fireplace.

Framing one side of the Place de la Liberté, the Hôtel de Ville succeeded in the seventeenth century a much older town meeting house. Later alterations have not been very successful. The northern end of the square is dominated by the bulky mass of the *Church of Sainte-Marie*. It was begun in the fourteenth century and completed in 1507. St Mary's was the parish church standing, with the Hôtel de Ville, at the centre of what was regarded as the 'town-end' of Sarlat, as opposed to the clergy-end around the cathedral and rivalry between the two would have been strong. Significantly, perhaps, the road that joins them—the Rue de la Liberté—was formerly the Rue Bourgeoise. In the Revolution, St Mary's became an arms factory; afterwards it was used as shops, a post office and, finally, a dispensary. Stone and timber were removed and used in other buildings but the bell tower was saved and the foreshortened church was eventually restored after World War I. The streets behind St Mary's are all worth exploring for their wealth of architectural detail. Of the many distinguished town houses there, the *Hôtel Plamon* in the Rue des Consuls is the most striking. Begun in the fourteenth century by a family who were prominent in local affairs, it was altered and added to as the family prospered so that its façade alone spans several centuries.

Returning to the Place de la Liberté, the Rue de la Salamandre rises steeply from the square, illustrating the problems posed by the site of Sarlat. In this narrow lane the houses have fairly recently been restored and the *Hôtel Saint-Aulaire* has an elegant staircase tower which is entered through a beautifully sculptured doorway of the fifteenth century. Further up the hill, the *Présidial*—sixteenth-century equivalent of the law courts—presents a curious mixture of architectural ideas, but it has a pleasant garden and some attractive wrought-iron work. The Rue d'Albusse brings one to the Rue Montaigne which has many distinguished houses, and from it a path leads to a small garden and what must be the strangest building in Sarlat—the

*Lanterne des Morts.* Round, with a high conical roof, it dates from the twelfth century and is reputed to have been built to mark the return of Saint Bernard from his crusade against the Albigensian heretics. Its purpose has never been wholly proven but it seems likely that it served as some kind of funeral chapel or resting place for the dead; hence its name. Certainly it is close to the old cemetery, and 'catacombs'—tombs built into the wall behind the cathedral. From the Lanterne des Morts a path can be found leading through two courts, site of the abbey, back to the Rue Tourny.

To describe a short tour of certain streets may be helpful to the visitor with little time to spare, but inevitably it leaves many gaps. No reference has been made, for example, to that part of Sarlat west of the Traverse where the very narrow streets converging on the Rue des Trois Conils have great atmosphere and appeal. Like the best pâté and wine, Sarlat must be savoured slowly to appreciate its distinction.

## NONTRON

Nontron has a more dramatic site than any other town in Périgord. Perched on a narrow promontory of rock and flanked by gorges of the Bandiat and its tributaries, it looks in one direction towards the high plateaux of Périgord Vert and, in the other, across a small fertile basin to the limestone hills of Périgord Blanc. The Bandiat, after flowing in a valley carved deeply into the granite plateau, makes a sharp bend to the west as it enters the more easily eroded belt of Jurassic clays and limestones. Within the angle of the bend, it is joined by a small, but equally deeply incised tributary isolating between itself and the Bandiat the narrow fringe of plateau on which Nontron stands. The defensive possibilities of the site are obvious and a castle was built on the edge of the rocky peninsula overlooking the gorge of the Bandiat. The present château was rebuilt in the eighteenth century but parts of the old fortifications remain.

The commercial spine of Nontron, the Grande-Rue, follows the ridge of the plateau and overlooks the old town clinging to its slopes. Seen from the *place* above, the old town presents a confused but highly picturesque array of roofs and little terraced gardens, almost filling the tributary valley to the west. The approach to the centre of Nontron was once by narrow lanes which wound their way up the plateau amongst these old houses, but the task of the modern motorist has been made easier with the construction of viaducts. Two of these serve road traffic; a third carries the railway in a graceful curve across the Bandiat. Beyond the railway the valley opens out and there is room for sports fields, stadiums and camping grounds.

As a market town, Nontron owes its importance to its position at the meeting place of contrasting pays. It is close to the boundary between Périgord, Limousin and Angoumois which has given the town an added strategic significance over the centuries. At the present day, like Bergerac and Sarlat, it has the status of sous-préfecture although its population is little more than 4,000.

The fast-flowing Bandiat and its tributaries have provided abudant waterpower, not only for grain and sawmilling, but also for a range of manufacturing industries. Nontron was formerly the commercial centre of the iron industry (page 83), and an interest in metals survives in the form of a highly specialised knife-making industry for which the waterpower of the river has been a particular advantage. High-quality steel is used for the blades and the handles are made of boxwood, engraved in a traditional pattern. Miniature knives are also a speciality. Another distinctive industry, and one which employs large numbers (about 800), is the manufacture of slippers. Nontron is one of the leading centres of this industry in France, responsible for a fifth of the national production, and there are about a dozen factories. In contrast with slippers, Nontron also makes clogs, including their metal runners. In addition, tourism is a rapidly expanding activity. With its woodland and lakes, river gorges and rocky outcrops, the Nontronnais attracts large numbers of visitors for whom Nontron itself acts as the natural service centre.

### RIBÉRAC

No better example than Ribérac can be found of the small country town which typifies rural France. It has few buildings of any distinction. The castle under whose wing the town sheltered has completely disappeared; the old church offers little of interest and the new one is nineteenth-century Byzantine; many of the older houses were pulled down when the streets were widened, also in the last century. The town is no longer a sous-préfecture; the railway has closed, and there is little employment in manufacturing apart from that provided by a small weaving and clothing industry. Yet Ribérac is always busy and animated and on Friday market day the streets and squares throng with crowds who have come in from the farms and villages of Périgord Blanc, the Double, or even further afield. The shops, banks and other services of Ribérac cater for a growing number of visitors, many of whom are English and own cottages in the district, but the town (population 4,100) has not lost its traditional role of serving the local farm community, and on Friday morning there is no more natural or genuine place than this in the whole of the Dordogne.

In the ninth century a defensive fort was established on the left bank of the Dronne to guard the river crossing from attacks by Vikings. The fort, or château, gave its name to the riverside suburb of Ribérac known as Le Chalard, but the actual town grew up a few hundred metres to the south in a minor tributary valley where the seigneurial manor was built on a limestone bluff. For centuries the life of the town was closely bound up with the fortunes of the 'big house'. Freed from feudal domination, Ribérac emerged in the nineteenth century as the commercial centre of the surrounding area—the Ribéracois—profiting from the many roads that converge on the crossing of

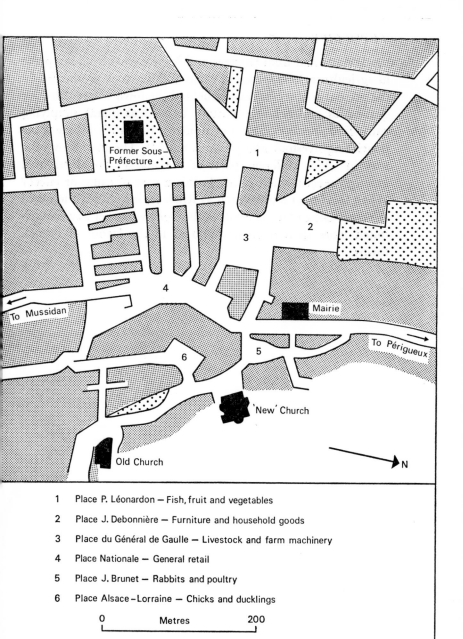

1   Place P. Léonardon – Fish, fruit and vegetables

2   Place J. Debonnière – Furniture and household goods

3   Place du Général de Gaulle – Livestock and farm machinery

4   Place Nationale – General retail

5   Place J. Brunet – Rabbits and poultry

6   Place Alsace-Lorraine – Chicks and ducklings

0          Metres          200

Fig 16   Ribérac and its market

the Dronne and from changes and improvements taking place in agriculture. The spread of grain and livestock production in the present century has also benefited the town where there are grain silos and a large abattoir, as well as plants supplying cattle feed and agricultural equipment. In addition there is the flourishing livestock and produce market. The map shows the way in which different parts of the market are distributed amongst several small *places*. Is this a case of cause or effect? When looking at a town such as Ribérac, it is difficult to avoid the conclusion that the needs of the weekly market have contributed more than is often supposed to the layout of French towns.

*Page 207*
Sarlat:
(*left*) Rue de
la Liberté
and the
tower of
Saint-
Sacerdos;
(*right*)
Lanterne
des Morts

*Page 208  (above)* Folk dancers in regional costume: the 'Cardils' dancing the
'Pélélé' in Paris; *(below)* village wedding in the Dordogne: the bridal party walk
on a path of moss and flowers *(la jonchée)* to the church

# 10 GASTRONOMY AND TOURISM

IN a country famed for its cuisine, the Dordogne region has an outstanding reputation for food, meriting the title *royaume de gueule*—literally translated as kingdom of the mouth—accorded to it by no lesser an authority than the *Guide Michelin*.

The rich pâtés of Périgord have long been renowned, yet as the novels of Eugène Le Roy make abundantly clear, the ordinary peasant family was, even to the early part of the present century, often reduced to a state of near starvation. In this seeming paradox lies the secret of Périgord's gastronomic fame, for it is based not on the products of the wealthy farmer —meat and grain—but on the variety of small articles, some home-grown, many gathered in the woods, which helped sustain the poor peasant: poultry, vegetables and fruits, but also fungi, nuts, game, herbs and, of course, garlic. Some of these would be the basis of the thick soup which would be the first, and sometimes the only, course in the peasant family meal and the call to table in the Dordogne— 'Faire Chabrol'—is based on a custom associated with this traditional soup dish. When the soup is almost finished some red wine is poured into the dish and stirred into the remains of the soup. Then the whole is drunk from the dish. Le Chabrol is said to be good for ailments of the throat and stomach but one need not be ill to enjoy it!

Few farms in Périgord are without their small flock of geese, as we have seen, and because it is the source of so many good things, the goose must be regarded as a kind of symbol of all that is best in Périgord cuisine. It is rarely eaten in the form of roast goose, however, as one might eat it at Christmas in Britain, for it tends to be too fat. However, after being cooked and then preserved in its own juice, it is served as *confit d'oie* and eaten either hot or cold. *Cassoulet* is a rich stew which includes pork, sausage and beans as well as preserved goose, but it is a more common dish in the area around Toulouse than in Périgord.

Goose liver is, of course, the basis of the very best pâté de foie gras and its fat is widely used in cooking. Other forms of poultry—chicken, duck, turkey or guinea fowl—as well as pork and rabbit, also enter into confits and pâtés, and local variations in the method of preservation mean that there is an enormous range of dishes to savour. *Confit d'oie à la sarladaise*, for example, is a preserve which uses potatoes and truffles. Portions of truffle are used to impart extra flavour and aroma to the best confits and pâtés, but these are not cheap. For the price of a single portion of pâté de foie gras one might buy untruffled pâté de volaille, a freshly baked baguette and locally-grown tomatoes sufficient for an enjoyable picnic for the whole family.

The truffle is enormously versatile. In addition to its use in pâtés, it enters into sauces, omelettes and salads and it is the basis of the stuffings which play an important part in Périgord cooking. It has rightly been described as the soul of Périgord cuisine. But although it is the most valuable, the truffle is not the only fungus eaten and the *cèpe*, for example, a variety of edible toadstool which appears in early and late summer, contributes to a number of popular dishes including *omelette aux cèpes*. Those who like mushrooms on toast will enjoy *la croute aux morilles*.

In the past, necessity often turned peasant into poacher and skills acquired in preparing rabbit, hare and game for the table have left their mark on local cooking. Dishes such as *lapin farci braisé* (braised rabbit with stuffing), *civets de lièvre* (jugged hare) and *lapin aux verjus* (rabbit cooked in grape juice) give an idea of the versatility of approach that arose from a need to exploit whatever came to hand. Such, too, must have been the origin of a dish like *surprise de gibier Périgueux* which uses quail, thrushes and boned larks with a stuffing of mushrooms and truffle. For those who feel unhappy about eating small birds it is possible to make do with pheasant, partridge or pigeon.

Vegetables eaten with many of these dishes include the universal petits pois and haricots verts (which may be called *mounzettas*), but also salsify—a plant with a fleshy root—asparagus and even chestnuts in the form of a purée. Potatoes are served more commonly than in many parts of France and in several forms, for example as *pommes rissolées, à l'échirlette, paysannes* or *sarladais* (a potato pie). Then there is *mique*, a kind of dumpling which is made from a mixture of maize and wheat flour, eggs and lard, and eaten with a meat stew. But many versions of mique will be encountered and in some places it may even turn out to be a cake. Local families often observe 'le jour de la mique', another relic perhaps of the days when meat was in short supply. *Tourteaux* are a kind of pancake made from maize flour.

Périgord has been described as a land of four rivers and these and their tributaries afford a variety of fish which, like the game, has long been used to supplement the peasant diet. They may appear on the modern menu as, for example, grilled trout, perch or tench; pike or carp cooked on the spit; fried gudgeon; eels served in red wine; or crayfish. The latter are common in streams which are highly charged with calcium carbonate since they take up lime from the water for their shells. The river Beune which joins the Vézère at Les Eyzies is one such river, draining an area of highly soluble limestone.

The Dordogne is not renowned for its cheeses although it is often possible to obtain a delicious cream cheese direct from the farm or in the market. For dessert, however, there is a wide range of locally grown fruit and nuts. The former include plums, cherries, apricots, peaches, pears, strawberries and table grapes (*chasselas*), some of which go to make the delicious tarts without which no Sunday lunch would be really complete. Anyone who likes nuts will enjoy the walnuts of this region, so much juicier when eaten in Périgord it seems than after they have been exported. They also yield oil which is used both for cooking and in salads, and they are the basis of a rich liqueur called *crème de noix* or *la vieille noix*. It is hardly surprising that the walnut tree is so highly valued or that such care is taken over its grafting on the occasion when a new one happens to be planted. The edible chestnut may be less important than in the past when flour made from the nuts was a standby if the cereal crop failed, but pigs are still fed on the nuts and the grafted varieties yield chestnuts for roasting and for use in soups, purées and stuffing.

Many farmers in Périgord make their own wine and also distil a little *eau de vie* which becomes a base for making delicious liqueurs from plums, blackcurrants and other fruits or berries. The *propriétaire* who presses his own wine will always swear that it is better than that from a co-operative which is likely to be *truqué* (adulterated) to the extent of one glass of water to the bottle of wine. If there is any water in his wine it is because there was a shower of rain when the grapes were being picked. Named wines, as opposed to these home-produced kinds, are made from grapes grown in the Bergeracois. Most famous of these is Monbazillac, a sweet white wine with a distinctive bouquet. Vineyards to the north of the Dordogne yield other well-known wines, including the fine white Montravels, Le Rossette—mellow, fruity, and also white—and the full-bodied, red Le Pécharmant. Other wines, usually served as *vins du pays* and including both reds and whites, are produced from vineyards which grow on the valley plain.

Most of the hotels in Périgord are small, family-run businesses. Le patron does the cooking, perhaps with one or a couple of young assistants depending on the size of the establishment; Madame supervises the dining-room and, if they are old enough, her children may help the couple of girls who come in from the village to serve; Grand'mère looks after *l'addition* (the bill) and sees to the late traveller seeking a room. The atmosphere is friendly and informal, yet great pride is taken in the quality of the food and in serving it correctly, and this applies as much to the cheapest menu as to the menu gastronomique. Indeed it is to the former, the *plat du jour*, that Monsieur will have given most thought that same morning in the market. The visitor to Périgord will need little persuading that good eating is still re-garded as part of a way of life and that food is something to be savoured and, wherever possible, enjoyed in the company of one's friends.

> Périgord isn't just a region where one eats well, it is a land where one eats in style and where the preparation of a meal is regarded as one of the fine arts.
>
> André Maurois

### TRADITION AND FOLKLORE

Like the Eisteddfod in Wales, *La Félibrée* is held annually in a different town or village in Périgord, always on the first Sunday in July. It is a gathering of those who seek to preserve the old language, customs and dress of the region, and the day is given over to songs, dances, processions and, of course, eating. Thanks to events of this kind, there is a strong revival of interest in the past.

The regional dialect, the *langue d'oc*, language of the trouba-dours, passed out of use amongst the educated section of the population as Périgord became politically integrated into a France dominated by the North where 'French', the *langue d'oïl*, was spoken. But it survived in the countryside where dialect phrases can still be heard and now its study has been revived, and the subject can even be offered as an option in the *baccalaureat* examination. Périgord was the northern limit of the langue d'oc and, in fact, two forms were spoken, a Limousin dialect which was used in the northern and central parts of the region and has soft consonants and endings (*catégna* for chestnut) and a southern, or gascon, form spoken in the Sarladais and the Bergeracois where the sounds were harsher (*lo cohtègno*).

> Ne leissas pas la vielho fado
> Mouri entau abandounado
> Qu'ei l'âmo de chas nous, la vou de notra soù
> Gardas la coumo un eiretage

Folklore societies have done much to preserve a knowledge of regional costume and this interest extends even to Paris these days, where emigrés Périgordins can belong to an association known as *Les Périgordins de Paris* which organises folklore evenings and other events with a regional flavour. The traditional costume for men consists of a dark blue smock which is worn over a thick, woollen waistcoat or short coat. A yellow and red necktie (*lo cor de côu*) is always worn and a broad-brimmed, black felt hat that protected its wearer from both sun and rain. For women, there is a tightly pleated jacket worn with a long skirt, gathered at the back, and a black apron with ample pockets. The headdress is of white linen or net with large flaps on the shoulder and, accompanying it, a broad collar of the same material. White gloves and stockings complete the costume. Village fêtes sometimes provide an occasion for bringing granny's old clothes out of the big, walnut chest, and market traders will occasionally dress in authentic costume to attract customers to their stalls.

Interest in regional affairs also extends to traditional crafts, especially those concerned with the foodstuffs for which the Dordogne is famous. Growth of the tourist industry helps to promote such an interest and it is a sign of the times that a shop —*La Maison du Périgord*—opened in Paris in 1968, devoted exclusively to the sale of articles made in this part of France.

'Périgord, terre de poésie', 'Périgord, capitale mondiale de la préhistoire', 'Périgord, terre d'élection du tourisme culturel'; phrases like these are frequently encountered in descriptions of the Dordogne which highlight the attraction of the region's varied landscapes and its wealth of historic sites and buildings. The castles and caves are real enough, drawing an increasing number of tourists to the region each year, but to the visitor the charm of the Dordogne lies equally in the unpretentious and 'unspoilt' quality of its life and in the 'home-spun' activities associated with that life.

The village fête is one of many essentially domestic events in which the visitor is welcome to share with the local population, and there are scores of them taking place during the summer months. Saint-Victor's is typical of the smallest fêtes, not even advertised in the calendar published by the *Office Départemental de Tourisme*. It takes place on a Sunday afternoon early in August; the streets are decorated with bunting; music is played over a loudspeaker, and in 1973, for example, the attractions were a roundabout for the children and two stalls offering a choice of breaking bottles or knocking over piles of tin cans. There was a sweet stall (it might have been crêpes); the village shop was selling the bags of confetti without which no fête would be complete, and already one or two girls were dancing in the village hall, although the dance would not really liven up until the evening. The streets were not entirely crowded but most of the villagers were there, together with a few who had come in from farms nearby, and the 'attractions' were all doing a brisk trade.

Other fêtes are more elaborate, perhaps lasting two days and ending with a torchlight procession and fireworks. Cycling, horse-riding or *moto-ball* (football on motorcycles) are likely to feature in a programme which these days will almost certainly include a parade of drum-majorettes, and possibly a brief visit from some well-known 'pop' idol. If there is a lake or river, the attraction will be a *concours de pêche* or *fête nautique*. Despite the obvious veneer of the 1970s, many of the fêtes have their origin in religious festivals or pilgrimages of considerable antiquity. The same is true of the fairs held in honour of some event or figure of the past.

During the summer months exhibitions of arts and crafts are staged in several village halls as well as displays illustrating local history and folklore. Following the restoration of its abbey church, Saint-Amand-de-Coly has become a centre favoured by artists and craftsmen. Elsewhere it is possible to see what is involved in traditional industries such as papermaking (at Couze), pottery (Mussidan) and weaving (Saint-Vincent-Jalmoutiers).

There are annual festivals of drama at Sarlat and of dancing at Brantôme, with concerts staged in many other small towns. Plays are also acted by travelling theatre groups, a popular theme being the life and times of Jacquou le Croquant. Information about all these events can be obtained from offices of that admirable French institution, the *Syndicat d'Initiative*. No fewer than forty-eight towns and villages in Périgord support such an 'S.I.', an indication of the wealth of interest of all kinds awaiting the visitor. Two publications which appear annually are also valuable guides to what is taking place: the special number of *Vacances Magazine* devoted to Périgord, and the summer holiday number of *Périgord Magazine*.

*Accommodation*

Périgord has few big hotels as a glance at the Michelin Red Guide will confirm. Yet there are many modest hostelries of the kind described on pages 212-13, whilst accommodation and a quite excellent meal can often be found in a village café, shop or even private house if the trouble is taken to inquire. It is, in fact, possible to arrange this kind of accommodation in advance by

216

obtaining a list of *Gîtes Ruraux* from the Office Départemental de Tourisme in Périgueux (16, Rue Wilson). Gîtes ruraux (literally, country lodgings) range from small farmhouses and 'typical' cottages to manor houses and even châteaux, and information about the facilities offered and how to rent them will be supplied with the list of addresses.

Farm holidays are also becoming popular, offering the best way of getting to know the people and their way of life. The local Syndicat d'Initiative will usually be able to help with addresses, but more general information can be obtained from the *Section Tourisme* of the *Chambre d'Agriculture de la Dordogne* in Périgueux (4–6, Place Francheville). This office also supplies information about camping or parking a caravan on the farm. For campers there are, in addition, a large number of well-organised sites, most of them in a pretty setting close to one of the region's major rivers.

*Buying a Cottage*

Continuing rural depopulation has meant that a large number of cottages and farmhouses have come on to the market as 'second homes'. Some have been bought by French families living in Paris, Bordeaux and elsewhere, but others have been sold to foreigners amongst whom the English have featured prominently, especially in the Ribéracois where prices have tended to be lower than in the better-known areas of the Dordogne valley and Sarladais. If population trends provide any clue, the best value in the future is likely to be found in the hillier country of the Nontronnais. Happily there is no resentment amongst the resident population of this new invasion by the English, and indeed it may be argued that the influx of home buyers is helping to preserve properties from decay. Certainly the work of restoring them has brought useful employment to many village craftsmen.

The difficulties involved in buying a property in the Dordogne are made easier by the willingness of estate agents to deal with English customers, and there are several English agents also working in the region. Some of these advertise in the Sunday press, and the prospective buyer would be well advised to obtain a copy of Raymond Crawford's *A House in the Dordogne* which describes all the stages involved in purchase and the structural problems likely to be encountered in the course of restoration.

Repairs and extensions to country cottages have not always been carried out in the past in sympathy with local architectural styles, and a purchaser wishing to do this kind of work will find that planning regulations are now being enforced to ensure a more harmonious result. A visit to the *mairie* is a useful first step in seeking planning permission. An organisation called *Sauvegarde du Périgord* has also been set up which offers advice on how to restore cottages without loss to their regional style.

### ONE MAN'S PROFIT

To the intending purchaser of a country cottage, rural depopulation is not the same problem that it is to the village shopkeeper or schoolmaster, a reminder that change should not evoke hasty judgements. Montaigne saw change always taking place at the expense of what had gone before and, as there is always change, so there is always a measure of loss which it is fruitless to lament.

Yet it would be over-sanguine to suggest that the Dordogne region of France is not faced with problems of adjustment to changing circumstances. Loss of population by migration is almost entirely limited to those under the age of forty, which has left the region with a higher proportion of old and fewer young people than in France as a whole. It is less easy for the elderly to change, to reorganise their farm holdings or to adapt to work in a factory. Thirty-five per cent of the working population is still employed in primary occupations, principally agriculture, more than double the national average. It would be surprising if this proportion could be maintained, however hopeful the progress now being made in farming, and it is significant that the greatest losses of population in the 1960s have been from the rural areas of the Nontronnais and the Ribéracois where big livestock enterprises can now be found.

Manufacturing employment is mostly confined to industries that are experiencing little or no growth and the industrial base is a narrow one. Typical are extractive industries—including the important cement works at Saint-Astier—and industries making shoes and slippers, paper, furniture and a variety of food products. Apart from railway engineering at Périgueux and the cellulose and plastics factories at Bergerac and Lalinde, the metal and chemical industries are barely represented. There are few big enterprises—the large, modern shoe factory of the Bata Group at Neuvic and the papermills at Condat are exceptional—and most works are small, employing under fifty workers and often fewer than ten. Their products find it difficult to compete with mass-produced goods made elsewhere. A number of small industrial estates have been set up, but success in attracting industries from outside the region has so far been limited. But that is not to say that it will never come. In a society tormented by noise, pollution and traffic, Périgord offers some attractions to the industrialist whose materials are not expensive to transport, and lack of coal is no longer a problem when hydro-electricity and natural gas can be supplied cheaply from other parts of the country.

The Dordogne is still a well-forested region but the forest poses a dilemma. Overall it is far from well managed, and most of the industries which make use of wood to manufacture paper or cellulose are forced to draw a large proportion of their raw materials from outside the region. Efforts are being made to utilise more of the local woodland, especially the chestnut forests, but to do so effectively would mean an ambitious programme of replanting that would create much more continuous stretches of forestland than at present exist. Inevitably this would give rise to conflicts of opinion over land-use and amenity. It would hardly seem to be the appropriate moment to plant extensive forests at a time when woodland is being removed for new crops such as strawberries and when tourism is such a valuable support to the regional economy. The furniture-making industry is profiting from the growth of tourism and the boom in cottage buying, and there may be more lessons to be learned from these activities that would serve to promote further uses for the woodlands.

The Périgordin is a complex personality, sociable but independent, superstitious but full of good sense, welcoming but distrustful of authority. He is an individualist, respecting freedom, yet easily feels concern for others, and in elections he expresses his outlook with a tendency to vote left—but not far left—of centre. It is unlikely that the attitudes that have maintained the integrity of Périgord for more than two thousand years will permit it to succumb easily to the pressures of the late twentieth century. His battle cry is not without its sense of humour:

*Petra* malis, *cor* amicis, hostibus *ensis*,
Haec tria si fueris, *Petrocorensis* eris.*

* A stone for the wicked, a loving heart for one's friends, a sword for the enemy— if you can find all three, you are a Périgordin.

# CASTLES OPEN TO THE PUBLIC

| | |
|---|---|
| BEYNAC | Dordogne valley<br>1 April to 30 September: 9.00–12.00; 14.30–19.00<br>1 October to 31 March: 10.00–12.00; 14.30–17.00 |
| BIRON | Near Monpazier<br>Palm Sunday to 30 September: 9.00–12.00; 14.00–18.00<br>1 October to Palm Sunday: 14.00–17.00<br>(closed February) |
| LES BORIES | Isle valley, east of Périgueux<br>1 July to 15 September: 10.00–12.00; 15.00–19.00 |
| BOURDEILLES | Dronne valley<br>All year: 9.00–11.30; 14.30–18.30<br>(closed 15 December to 15 January and on Tuesdays from 1 October to 30 June) |
| CASTELNAUD | Dordogne valley<br>1 July to 15 September |
| FAGES | Dordogne valley at Saint-Cyprien<br>1 July to 31 August: 9.00–12.00; 15.00–18.00<br>(closed Tuesday) |
| FÉNELON | Dordogne valley at Sainte-Modane<br>All year: 8.00–20.00 |
| HAUTEFORT | Largely destroyed by fire 1968. Gardens and courtyard can still be visited |
| L'HERM | Near Rouffignac, associations with Jacquou le Croquant<br>1 July to 30 September: 9.00–11.30; 14.00–18.00<br>(closed Friday) |

| | |
|---|---|
| JUMILHAC-LE-GRAND | Upper Isle valley, 20km from Thiviers<br>1 July to 30 September: 10.00–12.00; 14.00–18.00<br>Easter to 30 June: Sundays and feast days |
| LANQUAIS | Dordogne valley, west of Lalinde<br>All year: 9.00–12.00; 14.00–18.30 |
| MAREUIL | 20km north-west of Brantôme<br>Easter to 30 September: 10.00–12.00; 14.00–18.00<br>(closed Tuesday) |
| MONBAZILLAC | South of Bergerac, wine sold<br>All year: 9.00–12.00; 14.00–18.00 |
| MONTAIGNE | Dordogne valley, tower in which the essayist worked<br>All year: 9.00–12.00; 14.00–18.00<br>(closed January and on Mondays) |
| MONTFORT | Dordogne valley, south-east of Sarlat<br>Summer: 9.00–19.00<br>Winter: 10.00–15.00 |
| PUYGUILHEM | At Villars, north-east of Brantôme<br>All year: 9.30–12.00; 13.30–18.30<br>(closed Tuesday) |
| PUYMARTIN | Between Sarlat and Les Eyzies<br>1 July to 15 September: 9.00–12.00; 14.00–18.30 |
| SALIGNAC | 19km north-east of Sarlat<br>1 April to 31 October: 9.00–12.00; 14.00–19.00 |

# MUSEUMS

| | |
|---|---|
| BERGERAC | Tobacco Museum, in the Hôtel de Ville (history of the use of tobacco) Open Sundays: 14.30–16.30, during the week by request |
| BRANTÔME | Fernand Desmoulin Museum, in the Abbey (strange work of the local painter, Desmoulin, 1853–1914) Every day: 10.00–12.00; 14.00–17.00 |
| CHANCELADE | Museum of Diocesan Art, in the Abbey Every day: 14.00–18.00 |
| DOISSAT | Walnut Museum, 7km from Belvès |
| DOMME | Paul Reclus Museum (exhibition of prehistory) 1 April to 31 October: 8.30–12.00; 13.30–19.00 |
| EYMET | Archaeological Museum, in the Castle (prehistory and palaeontology) Open afternoons from July to September |
| LES EYZIES | Museum of Prehistory, in the Castle 1 April to 30 September: 9.00–12.00; 14.00–18.00 1 October to 31 March: 10.00–12.00; 14.00–18.00 Museum of Caving, on the road to Périgueux Open 1 July to 30 September |
| MONBAZILLAC | Museum in the Castle (Protestant history, furniture) Every day: 9.00–12.00; 14.00–18.00 |

## MUSEUMS

| | |
|---|---|
| MONTCARET | Gallo-Roman Museum, Dordogne valley near Montaigne (excavated Roman villa) |
| MONTIGNAC | Eugène Le Roy Museum (local history, including reconstruction of room in which the novelist worked) 1 July to 15 September: every day Easter to 1 July: Saturday afternoon, Sunday and public holidays |
| PÉRIGUEUX | Périgord Museum (prehistory collection of major importance) Every day: 10.00–12.00; 14.00–17.00 but closed Tuesday |
| | Military Museum, Rue des Farges (military objects from the Hundred Years' War to the Resistance) Open every day |
| SARLAT | Montaigne Gallery (exhibition of painting, engraving and sculpture) |
| THONAC | Centre of Prehistoric Art (life of early man, wildlife park) |
| VARAIGNES | Regional Museum, in the Castle (folklore, history and art) |
| VILLEFRANCHE-DE-LONCHAPT | Local History Museum, in the Hôtel de Ville |

# BIBLIOGRAPHY

### BOOKS

BARRÈRE, P., HEISCH, R. and LERAT, S. *La Région du Sud-Ouest*. Paris, 1962
BERESFORD, MAURICE. *New Towns of the Middle Ages*. 1967
CAUBET, JEAN. *Sarlat: Deux Mille Ans d'Histoire*. Sarlat, 1971
CHASSAING, MARC. *Images de Ribérac et du Ribéracois*. Ribérac, 1951
CHEYNIER, ANDRÉ. *Comment Vivait l'Homme des Cavernes à l'Age du Renne*. Paris, 1967
COLLECTION RICHESSES DE FRANCE. *Le Périgord*. Bordeaux, 1954
DANIEL, GLYN. *Lascaux and Carnac*. 1955
DUNSHEATH, PERCY. *Dordogne Days*. Woodbridge, 1972
ENJALBERT, HENRI. *Le Modèle et les Sols des Pays Aquitains*. Bordeaux, 1960
ESCANDE, J. J. *Histoire du Périgord*. Périgueux, 1934
FÉNELON, PAUL. *Le Périgord: Étude Morphologique*. Paris, 1951
FÉNELON, PAUL et al. *Guyenne*. Horizons de France, Paris, 1966
GALET, J-L. *Images Fantastiques du Folklore Périgordin*. Sarlat, 1963
——. *Connaissance de Périgueux*. Périgueux, 1972
GAUTHIER, J-S. *Les Maisons Paysannes des Vieilles Provinces de France*. Paris, nd
GRELIÈRE, PAUL. *La Dordogne: Ancien Périgord*. Périgueux, 8th ed, 1963
GUIDE DU PNEU MICHELIN. *Périgord, Limousin, Quercy*. Paris, 1961
HIGOUNET, CHARLES. *Histoire de l'Aquitaine*. Toulouse, 1971
LARTET, E. and CHRISTY, H. *Reliquiae Aquitanicae: Being Contributions to the Archaeology and Palaeontology of Périgord and the Adjoining Provinces of Southern France*. 1875
LAVERGNE, GERAUD. *Histoire de Périgueux*. Périgueux, 1945
LE ROY, EUGÈNE. *Le Moulin du Frau*. First published 1895; Les Editions du Périgord Noir, Périgueux, 1969

——. *Jacquou le Croquant.* First published 1899; Edition Livre de Poche, Paris, 1972

——. *L'Année Rustique en Périgord.* Les Editions du Périgord Noir, Périgueux, 1946

——. *L'Ennemi de la Mort.* First published 1913; Calmann-Lévy, Paris, 1959

MAUBOURGUET, JEAN. *Sarlat et Ses Châteaux.* Périgueux, 1960

——. *Domme et Pays Dommois.* Périgueux, 1973

MAUROIS, ANDRÉ. *Presentation du Périgord.* Les Albums des Guides Bleus, Paris, 1955

MICHEL, LÉON. *Le Périgord: Le Pays et les Hommes.* Périgueux, 1969

MONNERON, G. DE. *Nontron dans l'Histoire.* Périgueux, 1963

MONTAIGNE, MICHEL DE. *Essays.* Translated by J. M. Cohen, 1958

OYLER, PHILIP. *The Generous Earth.* 1950

PEYRONNET, E. *Les Anciennes Forges de la Région du Périgord.* Bordeaux, 1958

REBIÈRE, JEAN. *La Truffe du Périgord.* Périgueux, 1967

ROBERT, P. *L'Agriculture en Dordogne.* Bordeaux, 1958

ROCAL, GEORGES. *Croquants du Périgord.* First published 1932; presentation edition, Périgueux, 1970

——. *La Science du Gueule.* Presentation edition, Périgueux, 1970

ROUSSOT, ALAIN and FANLAC, PIERRE. *Périgord: Terre de Poésie.* Périgueux, 1971

SECONDAT, MARCEL. *Contes et Légendes du Périgord.* Périgueux, 1955

SECRET, JEAN. *La Dordogne de l'Auvergne au Bordelais.* Paris, 1962

——. *Châteaux en Périgord.* Paris, 1963

——. *Périgord Roman.* Paris, 1968

——. *Brantôme et Sa Région.* Périgueux, 1969

SEGOGNE, HENRY DE. *Dordogne: Trésors Touristiques de la France.* Périgueux, 1972

SYNDICAT D'INITIATIVE DE LA RÉGION BERGERACOIS. *Bergerac et Sa Région.* Bergerac, 1967

WHITE, FREDA. *Three Rivers of France.* 1962

PERIODICALS AND OTHER PUBLICATIONS

BALAGUER, MANUEL. *La Double de Dordogne.* Published by the author, nd

BONNICHON, J-E. *Regards sur l'Économie de la Dordogne.* Centre Départemental d'Études et d'Informations Économiques et Sociales, 1965

CHADEFAUD, MICHEL. 'Les Industries de Périgueux', *Rev Géog des Pyr et du S-O*, 1963, 405–9

CRAWFORD, RAYMOND. *A House in the Dordogne.* Published by the author, nd

DEFFONTAINES, P. 'Le Pays au Bois de Belvès', *Annales de Géographie*, 1930, 147–58

DEPAIN, MME. 'La Châtaigneraie Périgourdine', *Rev Géog des Pyr et du S-O*, 1936, 340–65

DICKINSON, R. E. *Les Eyzies and District.* Le Play Society, 1934

DU MÉO, GUY. 'Périgueux: la Population, l'Urbanisation Récente et Ses Problèmes', *Rev Géog des Pyr et du S-O*, 1971, 181–96

FÉNELON, M. P. 'Structure des Champs Périgourdins', *Bull de l'Assoc de Géographes Français*, 1939, 154–62

——. 'Les Reliefs Karstiques du Périgord', *Rev Géog des Pyr et du S-O*, 1968, 151–67

GENTY, MICHEL. 'Les Papeteries de l'Aquitaine du Nord-Est', *Rev Géog des Pyr et du S-O*, 1970, 277–302

LA DOCUMENTATION FRANÇAISE. *Monographie Agricole du Département de la Dordogne.* Paris, 1958

LAUGÉNIE, CLAUDE. 'La Culture du Noyer en Périgord', *Rev Géog des Pyr et du S-O*, 1965, 135–58

LAVAUD, ODETTE. 'La Vallée Périgourdine de la Vézère', *Annales de Géographie*, 1931, 144–52

LERAT, S. 'La Révolution Agricole en Périgord', *Rev Géog des Pyr et du S-O*, 1967, 369–72

LIVET, G. 'La Double', *Rev Géog des Pyr et du S-O*, 1942, 170–260

PIJASSOU, RENÉ. 'L'Ancienne Industrie du Fer dans le Périgord Septentrional', *Rev Géog des Pyr et du S-O*, 1956, 243–68

——. 'Un Bilan Économique du Périgord en 1960', *Rev Géog des Pyr et du S-O*, 1962, 385–94

——. 'Un Canton du Ribéracois: Verteillac', *Rev Géog des Pyr et du S-O*, 1965, 427–33

——. 'Structures Agraires Traditionnelles et Révolution Agricole dans les Campagnes Périgourdins', *Rev Géog des Pyr et du S-O*, 1966, 233–62

——. *Regards sur la Révolution Agricole en Dordogne.* Centre Départemental d'Études et d'Informations Économiques et Sociales, 1967

VIGIÉ, A. 'Les Bastides du Périgord', *Acad des Scs et Lettres de Montpellier*, 1907, 279–473

——. 'Les Bastides du Périgord et les Rôles Gascons', *Bull Soc Hist et Arch du Périgord*, 1920, 143–54

227

## MAPS

Most of Périgord appears on the *Carte Michelin*, sheet 75, Bordeaux–Tulle, 1:200,000. A small portion in the north, around Nontron, is on sheet 72.

All the sheets of the *Carte de France*, 1:100,000 series, published by the Institut Géographique National, are available and are reasonably up to date. Six sheets (H 17–19 and I 17–19) cover most of the region.

The 1:50,000 series is incomplete. Some recently revised sheets can be bought but there are gaps in the coverage of the region. For some areas, the sheets published in World War II, and partially revised since, are still available.

# ACKNOWLEDGEMENTS

I
T is ten years since I first spent any length of time in the
Dordogne. Since then I have returned as frequently as pos-
sible and my wife and I have joined the growing number of
English folk who own a cottage there—in our case, half of one.
Our thanks are due to Norman and Joy Pollock for helping to
make this possible and to our good friends in Les Bigoussies
who have made us so welcome. Amongst them I must single out
Louis and Adrienne Nadal for all their kindness. An evening
in their company provides memories that warm the chilliest
English winter.

It is impossible to discover everything about the Dordogne
when one's home and work is in England and inevitably a book
of this kind draws on the knowledge and research of others. I
hope the latter will accept the list of works quoted in the
bibliography as some acknowledgement of the help I have
obtained from them. I feel particularly indebted for ideas to
Professor Paul Fénelon, Monsieur René Pijassou and Professor
Maurice Beresford.

The photographs have been acknowledged separately but I
wish to thank a number of persons who gave me, not only
photographs or maps, but also helpful advice: Mademoiselle
Lucienne Coutou of Les Périgordins de Paris; Monsieur R.
Boucharel, president of the Fédération Départementale des
Chasseurs de la Dordogne; Monsieur A. Dorchies of the
Chambre d'Agriculture de la Dordogne; and Monsieur Alain
de Swarte, president of the Fédération Nationale de Sauvegarde des Maisons et Paysages pour la Défense de l'Environne-

*ACKNOWLEDGEMENTS*

ment Rural and editor of the journal *Maisons et Paysages:
Nature et Environnement.*

In preparing the book for publication I am grateful to Helen
Bromley for drawing the maps with great care and attention
to detail, to Diana Steer for her accurate typing, and to Peter
Masters and Christopher Jackson for their photographic skills
which turned my poor originals into presentable pictures.

# INDEX

*Page numbers in italics indicate illustrations*